# KEEP

## Daily Readings

# ON

## to Celebrate Life

# DANCIN'

## BY TIM HANSEL

CHARIOT
FAMILY
PUBLISHING

These pages are gratefully dedicated to some very special people who have "stood in the gap" (Ezekiel 22:30) when we needed it most. They chose to embrace us and in so doing demonstrated that God's grace has no boundaries. Without their tangible encouragement uniquely expressed through them, we might have literally lost everything. Their combined compassion became our WILD HOPE as well as the WIND BENEATH OUR WINGS: Ed and Lynn Bent, Don and Karen Berns, Al and Kathleen Caperna, Stan and Debbie Deal, Pete and Kathy Glade, Steve and Susan Gibbs, Bob "Barnabas" Haffey, Allen and Gary Levi, Coleman and Carol Luck, Rudy and Inga Markmiller, Orv and Shirley Mostad, John and Julie Mork, Wes and Jenny Mudge, Dain and Jean Paulsen, Andy and Carol Phelps, Chuck and Christine Rose, Richard and Marj Simons, Kenny and Jennifer Tedford, Jr., Charlie and Lucy Wedemeyer.

## Books by Tim Hansel

*Eating Problems for Breakfast*
*Holy Sweat*
*Real Heroes Eat Pizza*
*Through the Wilderness of Loneliness*
*What Kids Need Most in a Dad*
*When I Relax I Feel Guilty*
*You Gotta Keep Dancin'*

*Giver of life, creator of all that is lovely,*
*Teach me to sing the words to your song;*
*I want to feel the music of living*
*And not fear the sad songs*
*But from them make new songs*
*Composed of both laughter and tears.*

*Teach me to dance to the sounds of your world*
*and your people,*
*I want to move in rhythm with your plan,*
*Help me to try to follow your leading*
*To risk even falling*
*To rise and keep trying*
*Because you are leading the dance.*

*Author Unknown*

Chariot Family Publishing
Cook Communications, Colorado Springs, CO 80918
Cook Communications, Paris, Ontario
Kingsway Communications, Eastbourne, England

KEEP ON DANCIN'
© 1995 by Tim Hansel

Cover design by Steve Diggs & Friends
Edited by Catherine L. Davis
First printing, 1995
Printed in the United States of America
99 98 97 96 95     5 4 3 2 1

**Library of Congress Cataloging-in-Publication Data**
Hansel, Tim.
    [Selections. 1995]
    Keep on dancin' : daily readings to celebrate life / Tim Hansel.
        p.   cm.
    Selections from the books of Tim Hansel
    ISBN 0-7814-0282-4 (hc)
    1. Devotional calendars.    I. Title.
BV4811.H26    1995
241'.2--dc20                          95-38742
                                                    CIP

Acknowledgments continued on page 383.

# Introduction

For more than fifteen years, Tim Hansel's books have encouraged, inspired, entertained, and above all, challenged readers. This devotional book is a collection of his writings.

In 1974 Tim fell, upside down, into a six-stories-deep crevasse while mountain climbing in the Sierras. Miraculously, he was not killed. Rather, he was able to climb out and drive himself home. But the damage to his back and neck left him in debilitating pain and he is now permanently disabled.

Before his accident Tim founded Summit Expedition, a wilderness survival school. More recently, he founded Ignite, Inc., an organization dedicated to rekindling the inner fire of creativity, compassion, and commitment to Jesus Christ. Because of his own experience, some of Ignite's ministry is directed to the disabled or those living in chronic pain.

The 365 meditations in this book can be read consecutively, or selectively from sections whose themes fit your present needs.

# *Table of Contents*

# LOOKING
# TO THE
# SOURCE
# OF LIFE

❧

*But Jesus came and touched them. "Get up," he said. "Don't be afraid." When they looked up, they saw no one except Jesus. Matthew 17:7, 8*

I can vividly remember a series of Bible studies with a group of high-school students from San Francisco. We examined the basic theology and doctrine of the church. We explored the philosophical and theological positions of the church through history, debating the relevance of each to today's problems of hunger, nuclear weapons, and other ultra–complex situations. We explored how their subjects at school wove together with all the subtleties of Scripture.

Finally one morning a student raised her hand and said, "I'm really getting confused. Is it okay when I get lost in all of this stuff—*if I just look at Jesus?*"

❧ ————————————————————

*I look to You, Jesus, because You alone hold the keys to life.*

*Everything that goes into a life of pleasing God has been miraculously given to us by getting to know, personally and intimately, the One who invited us to God. The best invitation we ever received! We were also given absolutely terrific promises to pass on to you—your tickets to participation in the life of God after you turned your back on the world corrupted by lust.*
*II Peter 1:3,4 (The Message)*

Peter's second epistle states that we can actually participate in God's divine nature. If we are privileged to have this remarkable identity with the living God, then why shouldn't we be able to solve some of our problems through the resources of who He is? Being a Christian in no way guarantees that life will be easier or more "successful." Being a Christian simply guarantees each of us an inseparable link with the absolute Resource that can empower us in any circumstance.

*You are everything I need for whatever faces me today. You are my Absolute Resource, God.*

❁

*You discern my going out and my lying down;*
*you are familiar with all my ways. Psalm 139:3*

On one of our Summit Wilderness "Adventure in Fathering" courses, Robert, age six, wandered off to the edge of the forest. When he realized he was lost, Robert remembered that the instructors had said that if he got lost he should just sit down. Soon his grateful father found him sitting on a log, waiting.

"Dad," Robert said, "I wasn't worried, because I knew if I was lost you would come looking for me."

When we get lost on the inside, most of us start to panic. We wander from relationship to relationship, from activity to activity in an attempt to find our way. Perhaps what we need to do is just sit down. God will find us if we wait. Like the little boy who was lost in the woods, we can say, "Abba, I wasn't afraid, because I knew You would be looking for me."

❁ ─────────────────────────────────

*Abba, sometimes I feel like a child who has*
*wandered from the path. Thank You for not*
*letting me out of Your sight.*

✥

*Even to your old age and gray hairs I am he, I am he who will sustain you. I have made you and I will carry you; I will sustain you and I will rescue you. Isaiah 46:4*

I feel most intensely lonely when I try to fix the past or control the future. My mind wanders backwards to people and incidents which have caused someone pain . . . mistakes I have made or words that have hurt me. I review these in the movie of my mind, going over and over and over them.

At other times I fearfully look forward. Anxious about something that might happen, I try to manipulate people or circumstances to cushion the potential pain.

How strange we human beings are. We avoid what is, focusing instead on what might have been or what could be.

God, our only hope for healing, can be experienced in the present tense alone. His name is "I AM"!

✥ ─────────────────────────────

*How thankful I am that You are a present-tense God who holds both my past and my future in Your hand.*

❧

*Are you tired? Worn out? Burned out on religion? Come to me. Get away with me and you'll recover your life. I'll show you how to take a real rest. Walk with me and work with me—watch how I do it. Learn the unforced rhythms of grace. I won't lay anything heavy or ill-fitting on you. Keep company with me and you'll learn to live freely and lightly. Matthew 11:28 (The Message)*

The Bible says that this place we seek is a Person, that the peace that we look for is a presence rather than a principle. The simple truth is that we were made for God and therefore will never truly find rest anywhere else. This is a stubborn, profound, simple fact. Once we accept it with gratitude, we can return it with joy.

Isn't it interesting that Jesus says, "Come to Me"? Personally, if I had a choice (and I do) I would rather trust a person than a principle. I'd rather trust a reality than a rule. I'd rather trust a living truth than a theory.

❧ ——————————————————————————

*You said, "Come," and I do come to You, the One who understands heavy burdens and offers true rest.*

*Every God-begotten person conquers the world's ways. The conquering power that brings the world to its knees is our faith. The person who wins out over the world's ways is simply the one who believes Jesus is the Son of God.*
*I John 5:4, 5 (The Message)*

The Jesus I know leaks into the difficult places and joyfully overflows into problem places and people. He erupts into the geography of need, steals into the bruised crevices of hurt—the black-and-blue areas of pain. He is not safe. And when He fully invades a person by invitation, literally anything can happen. He doesn't come in to rearrange the furniture; He is into reconstruction. He doesn't repair, He recreates. He is not so interested in making us "religious" as in making us whole. He was considered dangerous to public safety when He walked this earth. Today this same Jesus is seeking men and women who will allow Him to be Himself—in all His fullness and unpredictability.

---

*Invade my life, Unpredictable One. Be Yourself in me today and overflow into the painful places.*

***Whatever God has promised gets stamped with the Yes of Jesus. In him, this is what we preach and pray, the great Amen, God's Yes and our Yes together, gloriously evident. God affirms us, making us a sure thing in Christ, putting his Yes within us. II Corinthians 1:19 (The Message)***

When my younger son, Josh, was little, he had been suffering from an earache. At bedtime, he and his mom decided to have a time of prayer. Mom would pray for Josh, and then Josh would pray for her. Mom prayed a simple, earnest prayer regarding Josh's earache.

A few minutes later, Josh looked back at his mom and announced, "He said, 'YUP.' "

"What?" his mom asked.

"We asked Jesus to take the pain away, and Jesus came into my ear and took the fire away. He said, 'YUP.' "

Jesus is the divine YES. He is the affirmation of all life. Invite Him into your life today in newer and simpler ways.

---

*Jesus, help me to be childlike in my trust of Your presence—Your "Yes!" in my life.*

*As far as the east is from the west, so far has he removed our transgressions from us. Psalm 103:12*

A priest in the Philippines had a woman in his parish who deeply loved God and claimed she had visions in which she talked with Christ. The priest was skeptical, so to test her, he said to her, "Let me ask you a favor. The next time you have a vision, I want you to ask Christ what terrible sin I committed when I was in seminary."

No one knew about this sin that was a great burden of guilt to him. He felt he could never be forgiven.

A few days later the priest said, "Well, did Christ visit you in your dreams?"

"Yes, He did," replied the woman.

"And did you ask Him what sin I committed in seminary," he asked rather cynically.

"Yes, I asked Him."

"Well, what did He say?"

"He said, 'I don't remember.' "

---

*Help me remember, Jesus, that while I cling to my sins and wallow in guilt, you have banished them from Your sight.*

❧❧

*If any of you lacks wisdom, he should ask God,
who gives generously to all without finding fault,
and it will be given to him. James 1:5*

The primary core of all problem solving is
our attitude. We need to go after Moby Dick
with a harpoon and tartar sauce. Avoiding problems only amplifies them. Jesus is the divine *Yes*,
and we must not forget that! He is available to
assist us in our attitude and perspective, and can
use our problems to stretch, challenge, and
deepen our walk with Him. If we lack any wisdom (or if our attitude or perspective is distorted), we simply need to ask Him, and He has
promised to provide graciously and liberally.

❧❧ ───────────────────────────────

*You know the problems I am facing today, Jesus.
Thank You for Your promise of a generous
supply of wisdom.*

*The Lord replied, "My Presence will go with you, and I will give you rest." Then Moses said to him, "If your Presence does not go with us, do not send us up from here." Exodus 33:14, 15*

Contemplation and prayer must always precede action. A friend reminded me that Moses said in essence in the verse above, "If You ain't going with me, God, I ain't movin'."

We must receive before we can give. Once we open the door, God can go to work. That God should wait for our permission to bestow such wonderful gifts on us requires an almost preposterous humility on God's part and a preposterous openness on our part.

If some of us feel unqualified, it's because we are. We are absolutely unqualified to do God's work. Only He can do it within us. We are simply invited to be God's people—whoever we are, wherever we are.

*Lord, I accept the invitation to be Your person, knowing that Your presence will make it possible.*

❦

*If anyone acknowledges that Jesus is the Son of God, God lives in him and he in God. And so we know and rely on the love God has for us. God is love. Whoever lives in love lives in God, and God in him. I John 4:15, 16*

Want more passion in your life, more zest? Then put more into yourself and your relationship with God.

Self–love is too often confused with vanity and pride. We think it's selfish to love ourselves, when in reality it is selfish *not* to love ourselves. When we don't love ourselves we take from others in order to fill our own emptiness. The better I feel about myself, the better I usually feel about my relationships.

All of our relationships with people begin with our relationship with God. Christ has shown Himself among us. God has made His dwelling place within us. And this is what sets us free to love each other.

❦ _____

*Oh God, love this world through the person You have created me to be.*

*How great is the love the Father has lavished on us, that we should be called children of God! And that is what we are! I John 3:1a*

Through the simplicity of children God reminds us of the important things in life.

One evening at dinner my four-year-old son was so overtaken by the day that he was singing a little homemade song: "I was walking along and saw a dog—and he said bow wow. And the cat said meow, and the cow said moo. And I was walking along and I saw some flowers . . . "

There was a rather long pause, so I asked innocently, "And what did they say?"

"And they said, 'Jesus loves me, this I know, for the Bible tells me so.' "

When you are four, God is everywhere, and He is love.

*Dear Father, like a trusting child, help me to experience the reality of Your love for me.*

❧

*To them God has chosen to make known among
the Gentiles the glorious riches of this mystery,
which is Christ in you, the hope of glory.*
*Colossians 1:27*

Paul tells the Colossians that the central
mystery of the gospel is "Christ in you." This is
good, in fact, astonishing news: *Christ in you.*
Christ is not merely for us; He is in us.

Richard Halverson said, "When Christ was
on earth, He was limited by time and space. In
His body, He couldn't be two places at once.
Think how wonderful it would be to multiply
the presence of Christ by a million, or 10 million, or 100 million. That's the substance of this
mystery. . . . Wherever Christians are present,
Christ is present—not only with them, but in
them."

❧ _____

*Sometimes the wonder of Your indwelling presence
is astonishing to me. Wherever I am, there is the
presence of Christ!*

**Then their eyes were opened and they recognized him, and he disappeared from their sight.**
**Luke 24:31**

A camp counselor of junior high boys approached the cabin and heard an uproar that was probably audible in the next state. He walked up and stood outside the doorway a few moments, silently observing the rambunctious pillow fight taking place. Then he heard one of the kids say, "He's coming. He's coming. He's coming!" The boy's voice got louder as he tried to warn the others of the impending presence of their counselor.

There was a pause, and then one of the kids saw him in the doorway and said, "He's here! He's h-e-r-e!"

What a wonderful illustration of our relationship with God. Many Christians proclaim frequently, "He's coming! He's coming!" But they fail to recognize that He's here! He is here . . . if we can but recognize His presence.

*Oh, God, help me recognize You in the details of this day.*

❖

*Sing unto the Lord; for he hath done excellent
things: this is known in all the earth. Cry out
and shout, thou inhabitant of Zion: for great is
the Holy One of Israel in the midst of thee.*
*Isaiah 12:5, 6 (KJV)*

When I was little, our Boy Scout troop
went to Bainbridge Island for a weekend camp
out. On the second day we had a ferocious
game of hide-and-seek. I discovered a great hiding place in the ivy next to the big house.

It was so great that the others got tired and
stopped looking for me. Finally I hung my red
bandanna out on one of the branches. One kid
found the bandanna . . . but he never saw me.

What a picture this is of much of our lives.
Often we don't find what we're looking for
because we don't look at what is close to us. We
don't find God because we are only looking for
Him in faraway places. God is hidden in our
midst, if we could only see Him.

❖ ─────────────────────────────

*Lord, You are not a faraway God. You are always
present in the midst of my life. Thank You.*

❉

*Delight yourselves in the Lord; yes, find your joy in him at all times. Have a reputation for gentleness, and never forget the nearness of your Lord.*
*Philippians 4:4, 5 (Phillips)*

How close is God? He is closer than our breath. He is closer than our skin. How much does He care for Us? Scripture reminds us:

- *He knows our names (John 10:3).*
- *He numbers the hairs on our heads (Matthew 10:30).*
- *He counts the steps of our feet (Job 14:16).*
- *He bottles the tears from our eyes (Psalm 56:8).*
- *He holds our right hands in His hand (Psalm 73:23).*
- *He supplies all our needs (Philippians 4:19).*

❉ ———————————————

*You are nearer than breath and skin, Lord. Your great love and care is more than I can fathom. You are my joy and delight.*

❧

*And ye are complete in him, which is the head
of all principality and power.
Colossians 2:10 (KJV)*

I can trust God with my future, which not only means eternal life, but the next day, the next hour, the next ten minutes. Filling our emptiness is an inside–out–job. It means letting Him fill our loneliness with a fullness that we will never comprehend and only He can give.

Advertisements shout, "You need more. Your life is not enough." God whispers in the midst, "I am here. I am sufficient in your weakness. I am enough. In Me you are complete."

In Christ there is an uncrowded fullness. In Him there is an unhurried completeness. In Him is a whole number. In Him, enough is enough.

❧ _____

*Oh Christ, You are enough. You are all I need. Fill
the empty places of my life with Your presence.*

*On that day you will realize that I am in my Father, and you are in me, and I am in you.*
*John 14:20*

In the Indian language there is a greeting, *Namaste*, which means "I honor the holy one who lives within you."

Sometimes loneliness stems from not honoring the Holy One who lives within us. If you have invited Christ into your life, He does, in fact, dwell within you. Likewise, we must learn how to honor the Holy One within each other, so that we do not seek to use people simply to fill our emptiness.

Like a headlight that can only reach so far into the darkness, human love by its very nature has its limits. Our focus instead needs to be on the One who said, "I am the way, the truth, and the life."

*Holy One, remind me that You live within me when I am tempted to look to another person to meet my needs.*

❀

*Seek ye the Lord while he may be found, call ye upon him while he is near. Isaiah 55:6 (KJV)*

I am caught in L.A. traffic. There are people all around me, yet I feel so alone. We stop and start and pass each other by without even noticing. Radios blare, but there is no communication between us.

I'm suffocated by all the people, yet stifled by my own loneliness. Bumper-to-bumper sadness. Bumper-to-bumper loneliness. How strange that as the world grows ever more heavily populated, our depth of loneliness increases.

To ease the pain of loneliness, there must be connection. Connection with ourselves. Connection with others. Connection with God.

❀ ————————————————————

*When I feel disconnected from life, from others, even from You, You are there calling me to Yourself.*

❀

*You are not your own; you were bought at a
price. Therefore honor God with your body.
I Corinthians 6:19, 20*

A boy was very sad when he lost a boat
he had built by himself. One day he saw the
boat in a pawnshop window. He ran into the
store crying, "Mister, mister, that's my boat!"

The pawnshop owner said, "I'm sorry, son,
but that's my boat now. It will cost you two dollars and fifty cents to get it back."

Determined to get his boat back, the boy
finally earned the $2.50 and took it to the
pawnshop. On the way out the door, the boy
hugged the boat and said, "Little boat, you are
twice mine. I made you, I lost you, and then I
bought you back again."

God has a legitimate claim to our lives
because we are twice His. He made us, He lost
us, and then, through His Son, He bought us
back again.

❀ ⎯⎯⎯⎯⎯⎯⎯⎯⎯⎯⎯⎯⎯⎯⎯

*Such love, Lord. You made me for Yourself,
and then when I was lost from You,
You paid to get me back.*

❊

*I trust in God's unfailing love for ever and ever.*
*Psalm 52:8b*

One day, while my son Zac and I were out in the country climbing around in some cliffs, I heard a voice from above me yell, "Hey Dad! Catch me!" I turned around to see Zac joyfully jumping off a rock straight at me. He had jumped and then yelled "Hey Dad!" I became an instant circus act, catching him. We both fell to the ground. For a moment after I caught him I could hardly talk. When I found my voice again I gasped in exasperation: "Zac! Can you give me one good reason why you did that???"

He responded with remarkable calmness: "Sure . . . *because you're my Dad.*" His whole assurance was based in the fact that his father was trustworthy. He could live life to the hilt because I could be trusted. Isn't this even more true for a Christian?

❊ ———————————————————————

*I can fling my life into Your arms, God,*
*because You are utterly trustworthy.*

❧

*He is not here; he has risen, just as he said.*
*Come and see the place where he lay.*
*Matthew 28:6*

Johnny had a terminal disease and not long to live. His disease made it difficult for him to understand classroom assignments. During Easter the children were supposed to take an empty plastic egg and put something in it that reminded them of Easter.

The day the eggs were turned in, the teacher opened each one and made a positive comment. One egg was empty.

Johnny raised his hand. "Teacher, you didn't share mine."

"I'm sorry, Johnny. You were to bring something that means Easter to you, and put it in the egg."

"But Teacher," Johnny said, "Jesus' tomb was empty—and that's what Easter is all about."

Johnny died a few weeks later, and in his casket his classmates placed twenty-seven empty eggs. They understood.

❧ _____

*My heart is full, Risen Christ,*
*because Your tomb is empty.*

*The Lord appeared to us in the past, saying: "I have loved you with an everlasting love; I have drawn you with loving—kindness."*
*Jeremiah 31:3*

Some of us in our loneliness try to become more attractive so that we will be more lovable. We think that will somehow heal us, make us whole, make us real. The truth is that we need a Love that lasts for a long, long time from Someone who is not playing with us, but really loves us. So He heals us bit by bit.

When our striving fails, He is a God who comes to find us—even when we can't find ourselves. All too often we think we have to change, be good, to grow in order to be loved. In truth we are loved in order to change and grow and be all the things that God wants us to be.

*Lord, with Your loving—kindness, heal me bit by bit until I'm whole and real.*

*This is too glorious, too wonderful to believe! I can **never** be lost to your Spirit! I can **never** get away from my God. Psalm 139:6, 7 (TLB)*

Where are you missing God in your life? In which areas of your life are you having the most difficulty finding His presence and promise? Are you able to recognize His work in and through you in the midst of your loneliness or in the midst of some crisis you are facing? Write down ten places or areas of your life where you may be overlooking Him.

Then (and I hope this is as powerful for you as it has been for me) read Psalm 139 (preferably in *The Living Bible*) slowly and carefully, absorbing the incredible truth that you can never get away from God even if you try.

*Help me to see You, Lord, in those difficult places in my life. I know You are there.*

❀

*Search me, O God, and know my heart; test me and know my anxious thoughts. See if there is any offensive way in me, and lead me in the way everlasting. Psalm 139:23, 24*

Mike Mason says, "In each one of us the holiest and neediest place of all has been reserved for God alone, so that only He can enter there. No one else can love us as He does, and no one else can be the sort of Friend to us that He is."

Real love requires time, exposure, vulnerability, and commitment. The same is true of our relationship with God. If our love relationship with God is to grow, we must be ruthlessly honest with Him and let Him be ruthlessly honest with us. We must above all give Him time—time in which we can expose the real core of our being. We must dare to be real and open and vulnerable with Him.

❀ ———————————————————

*Don't let me hide myself from You, God. Give me the courage to open my heart to You in truth and honesty.*

✿

*"Am I only a God nearby," declares the Lord,*
*"and not a God far away? Can anyone hide in*
*secret places so that I cannot see him?" declares*
*the Lord. "Do not I fill heaven and earth?"*
*Jeremiah 23:23, 24*

A young man longed to see God. He had
heard of a wise old man who lived in the
mountains nearby. After searching elsewhere for
God in vain, the young man finally went to talk
with the old man.

"Old man, tell me, how can I see God?"

The old man looked at him deeply. He
immersed himself in thought. The young man
waited for what seemed like an eternity. Finally
the old man said, "Young man, I don't think
that I can be of help to you, for you see I have a
problem that is quite different. I can't *not* see
Him."

Grace washes away the imagined barriers
between secular things and spiritual things and
reintroduces the whole universe to us as God's.

✿ _____

*The whole universe is Yours, God! And You are*
*always present to me within my universe.*

❁

*But grow in the grace and knowledge of our Lord
and Savior Jesus Christ. To him be glory both
now and forever! Amen. II Peter 3:18*

Nothing can replace the power of a per-
sonal relationship with Jesus Christ. The
Christian life is not imitation, but habitation.
Christ in you is a continuous gift.

Two processes must live in constant fellowship with each other:

*Justification:* God accepts me as I am. (I do not
have to reform, improve my figure, or anything
else to come to Christ. He starts with me where
I am.)

*Sanctification:* God accepts me as I can be.
(Once I am justified, I am free to change, and
sanctification is the process of changing. God
takes me just as I am, but He will not leave me
that way—I'm in for a complete overhaul.)

We can no longer keep trying to cram God
into a junior–high camp experience.

❁ ———————————————————

*Thank You, my Savior, for accepting me for who
I am and who I can be. May Your life within
bring continuous growth.* ·

❀

*So don't be anxious about tomorrow. God will take care of your tomorrow too. Live one day at a time. Matthew 6:34 (TLB)*

> *Man's chief end is to glorify God
> and to enjoy him forever.*
> THE WESTMINSTER LARGER
> CATECHISM, 1861

One of the rarest species on the face of the earth may soon become extinct—those few human beings who truly know how to enjoy life.

They glorify God not only with their words but even more with their lives. They enjoy God for who He is, not just for what He can do for them. To them, each day holds its own reward. They know that each twenty–four hours is a once–in–a–lifetime privilege and that happiness is a by–product of quality living. Their lives are lived according to their priorities, in spite of the consequences. They have cracked through the thin crust we call civilization to find the super-natural substance upon which life rests.

❀ ———————————————————

> *Lord, You are the very substance of life.
> May this day bring glory to You.*

※

*Now this is eternal life: that they may know*
*you, the only true God, and Jesus Christ,*
*whom you have sent. John 17:3*

Robert M. Brown begins a chapter of his
*The Bible Speaks to You* with a scroll on which
are written the following words:

BE IT HEREBY ENACTED:

That every three years all people
Shall forget whatever they have learned
About Jesus,
And begin the study all over again.

While one great tragedy of the world is that
many people are unfamiliar with Jesus, it is
equally tragic that some of us are too familiar
with Him. We think we know, we think we
really understand the full significance of His life
within us and among us. But we trust a Person,
not a set of answers. And this Person is often
different from who we think He is.

※ ――――――――――――――――――――――

*Help me to see You in a new and fresh light, Jesus,*
*that I may once again be caught off guard by You.*

✵

*Grace and peace be yours in abundance through the knowledge of God and of Jesus our Lord. His divine power has given us everything we need for life and godliness through our knowledge of him who called us by his own glory and goodness. II Peter 1:2, 3*

Time and time again, throughout Scripture, God expresses His desire to give us *His* genuine strength and power. Paul reminds us that one of the greatest limiting factors to receiving that power is our temptation to rely on our own strength.

I've spent much of my Christian life thinking about what I could do for Jesus, rather than what He could do in me. Perhaps it is by God's grace that I'm no longer able to do all those things but must learn a new kind of receptivity, another kind of strength from a source which is not my own. In letting go—because I had to— I've discovered a more permanent kind of eternal peace and power.

✵ _____

*Eternal Peace and Power, forgive and transform my feeble attempts to live for You.*

❧

*Then a cloud appeared and enveloped them, and a voice came from the cloud: "This is my Son, whom I love. Listen to him!" Mark 9:7*

It was the middle of World War II. Men were giving their best on the front lines. Somehow one of them scrounged up an old beaten–up phonograph and a record of none other than Enrico Caruso, considered at that time the greatest singer in the world.

That evening as they sat around the tent listening to the scratchy, worn record on a weathered phonograph, there were two distinct groups of listeners. Some heard only the scratches on the record. Others, who listened more deeply, heard the master's voice.

Sometimes we can only hear the scratchiness of life. But if we will listen closely, we will hear the Master's voice. What is He saying to you?

❧ ———————————————————————

*In the scratchiness of life, help me to listen carefully for Your voice, Master of my life.*

❦

*God also said to Abraham, "As for Sarai your
wife . . . I will bless her and will surely give you a
son by her. I will bless her so that she will be the
mother of nations; kings of peoples will come from
her." Abraham fell facedown; he laughed and said
to himself, "Will a son be born to a man a hundred years old? Will Sarah bear a child at the age
of ninety?" Genesis 17:15–17*

One of Summit Expedition's exceptional
instructors, Rick Vander Kam, was asked . . .
"Hey, Rick, what are you going to be doing five
years from now?"

His answer is worth remembering. He began,
"I don't know."

To which his friend remarked, "What's the
matter? Don't you have dreams? Don't you have
goals? Don't you have plans?"

Rick answered, "Of course I do. I've written
down my goals and I've got incredible, specific
plans, but I happen to be following Somebody
who is *notoriously unpredictable*."

❦ _____

*Lord, I am grateful that, though I plan carefully,
You are in charge of the future.*

❧

*For this reason I kneel before the Father, from whom his whole family in heaven and on earth derives its name. I pray that out of his glorious riches he may strengthen you with power through his Spirit in your inner being. Ephesians 3:14–16*

This passage in Ephesians that begins with these verses is one of my favorites, for it reminds me of how much God wants to give us. It has been said that it is not so much our *ability* that counts as our *availability*. In Ephesians 1:19, 20 Paul says, "How tremendous is the power available to us who believe in God. That power is the same divine energy which was demonstrated in Christ when He raised Him from the dead and gave Him a place of supreme honor in Heaven." (Phillips)

We have available to us the veritable Easter power, but we can live out our whole Christian lives blindfolded to it if we've never really had to depend on His power and His power alone.

❧ ————————————————

*Lord, I want to be available to let Your astonishing power live out through me.*

*So the word of God became a human being and lived among us. We saw his splendor (the splendor as of a father's only son), full of grace and truth.*
*John 1:14 (Phillips)*

Some men named Matthew, Mark, Luke, and John tried to tell us of a man who left eternity and entered into time, and yet who walked within the boundaries of an eternal rhythm. They tried to tell us of the love that was beyond measure; a hope beyond reason; and a life–style that could have its source in an eternal rhythm. We have been told that this rhythm, this peace, this love, this joy can, in fact, be ours.

Little did they know, these Gospel writers, how busy we would be. Little did they know how important our work would be. Little did they know about our schedules and deadlines. But they told us about a life, the Life who lived according to a different timetable. Even in our day, the eternal beat goes on.

---

*You who are Life to me, may my heart beat to Your eternal rhythm.*

# THE
# POWER IN
# WEAKNESS
# AND PAIN

❋

*And the God of all grace, who called you to his eternal glory in Christ, after you have suffered a little while, will himself restore you and make you strong, firm and steadfast. I Peter 5:10*

In *Oh, God, Book II*, George Burns, playing the part of God, is asked by a tiny girl why bad things happen. Burns replies, "That's the way the system works. Have you ever seen an up, without a down? A front, without a back? A top, without a bottom? You can't have one without the other. It I take away sad, then I take away happy, too. They go together." Then, with a wry smile, he adds, "If somebody has a better idea, I hope they put it in the suggestion box."

*Oh, God, Book II* was never meant to be a theological film. But even in its comedy, it can remind us that the many sides of life are meant to fit together.

❋ ───────────────────────────────

*I would rather You took away sad and only left happy, God. But I know that I need the transforming power of suffering.*

❧

*Be merciful to me, Lord, for I am faint; O Lord,
heal me, for my bones are in agony. My soul is in
anguish. How long, O Lord, how long?*
*Psalm 6:2, 3*

Pain. It seems to be the common denominator of our human existence. It's part of the life experience. To avoid it is to detour the essence of life itself.

We all know what pain tastes like. Whether its source is physical, emotional, mental, or spiritual, its interruption in our lives disrupts and reshapes. It intercepts our hopes and plans; it rearranges our dreams. It always leaves a mark.

All of our lives are terminal. Only time and quality differ. The choice for all of us is not if we will accept pain, but how.

❧ ────────────────────────────────

*Lord, I don't want pain, but I know it is a
part of life. Help me to accept it and grow
through the experience.*

44

❧

*From the fullness of his grace we have all received one blessing after another. John 1:16*

We live in a world that is sometimes constipated by its own superficiality. But life's difficulties are even a privilege, in that they allow us or force us to break through the superficiality to the deeper life within.

Grace is the central invitation to life, and the final word. It's the beckoning nudge and the overwhelming, undeserved mercy that urges us to change and grow, and then gives us the power to pull it off.

*Break through the superficial crust of my life, Lord, and help me accept Your invitation to grow.*

✹

*But he knows the way that I take; when he has tested me, I will come forth as gold. Job 23:10*

When I became a Christian at Stanford University, I had strong, neat, crisp images of what my future was going to be like. I was going to be physically strong, for Christ's sake. I was going to be intellectually acute, emotionally bomb-proof, and spiritually profound—the very best that I could be to honor the Kingdom. But my story turned out differently than my original script.

Someone once asked a goldsmith how long he kept the gold in the fire. His reply: "Until I can see my face in it."

In His marvelous and mysterious way, God keeps shaping us until He can see Himself in our lives.

✹ ────────────────────────────

*Oh God, shape me until You can see Yourself in my life.*

❁

*And the peace of God, which transcends all understanding, will guard your hearts and your minds in Christ Jesus. Philippians 4:7*

I have a plaque, sent to me during a very difficult period of my life, that says the following:

*Tim,*
*Trust me. I have everything under control!*
*Jesus*

It was sent by a friend who knew that I needed that reminder. Ironically, the glass got broken during shipping. I have never replaced the glass because, to me, the message is even stronger behind shattered glass. We can know a joy that transcends circumstances and a faith that is beyond situations.

❁ ————————————————————————

*Beyond difficulty, beyond pain, beyond understanding, You are there with everything under control.*

❈

*I remember the days of long ago; I meditate on all your works and consider what your hands have done. Psalm 143:5*

St. Augustine said, "Lack of faith is not remembering what God has done for you in the past." Sometimes amidst pain, overwhelming grief, or undercurrents of sadness, it's difficult to remember how much God has done.

But one of the ways that our faith expresses itself is by our ability to be still, to be present, and not to panic or lose perspective. God still does His best work in the most difficult of circumstances. The Spirit is more powerful than the will, more powerful than the flesh, more powerful than pain, more powerful than guilt, even more powerful than our weakness and our doubt.

We can experience the living Christ here and now, and our difficult circumstances will be the very opportunity for our faith to grow.

❈ ————————————————————————

*When life overwhelms me, help me remember Your faithfulness and experience You once again.*

𝕊𝕃

*A week later his disciples were in the house again, and Thomas was with them. Though the doors were locked, Jesus came and stood among them and said, "Peace be with you!" Then he said to Thomas, "Put your finger here; see my hands. Reach out your hand and put it into my side. Stop doubting and believe." John 20:26, 27*

When God raised Jesus from the dead, the imprint of the nails could still be seen. Why didn't God fix Him up? Why did He leave the scars? Somehow we must understand that the resurrected Christ is the wounded Christ. Living, but never "fixed up." Not bound by death, yet scarred for eternity.

The deaf have a sign for Jesus. The middle finger of each hand is placed in the palm of the other. Jesus, the one with wounded hands.

We must find our wholeness in the midst of our woundedness. We must find peace in the midst of our loneliness. We cannot wait for the scars to go away.

𝕊𝕃 _____

*Help me to value my own scars as I see them reflected in Your nail—scarred palms.*

❋

*In future let no one make trouble for me, for I bear the marks of Jesus branded on my body.*
*Galatians 6:17 (NEB)*

Most of us want to be fixed, made okay, free from pain and loneliness. We want to be protected from the wounds of everyday living.

God is not going to take all the loneliness away and patch every hole in our lives. He is just going to give it meaning and purpose. He doesn't promise to fix us—just to make us whole and holy. St. Paul said, as he finished the letter to the Galatians, "I carry on my scarred body the marks of Jesus."

> *I said I found peace. I didn't say that I was not lonely.*
>
> ELISABETH ELLIOT

❋ _____

*Transform my wounds, Lord. Through Your grace make them a means of healing for others.*

*So he made a whip out of cords, and drove all
from the temple area, both sheep and cattle; he
scattered the coins of the money changers and
overturned their tables. To those who sold doves
he said, "Get these out of here! How dare you
turn my Father's house into a market!"*
*John 2:15, 16*

Feelings are at the heart of our relationship
to Christ—and to each other. Many of us have
learned to geld our feelings in order to fit in the
church. We've become emotional eunuchs so as
not to ripple the waters. Rather than risk the
splendor of real feelings, we have chosen to
reveal only those that are safe and sterilized,
pretested and acceptable. We have chosen a
"Christian reputation" over the risk of a genuine unpredictable relationship with Jesus
Christ.

*Lord, thank You that You already know my deepest
doubts, my nagging fears, the anger I can no longer
hide. And still You love me.*

❋

**For God so loved the world that he gave his one and only Son, that whoever believes in him shall not perish but have eternal life. John 3:16**

*"When a child loves you for a long, long time, not just to play with but REALLY loves you, then you become Real." "Does it hurt?" asked the Rabbit. "Sometimes," said the Skin Horse, for he was always truthful. "When you are Real you don't mind being hurt."*
The Velveteen Rabbit,
*by Margery Williams*

God's love is sometimes painful. Whereas the Valentine-Day kind of love is pictured as a heart with an arrow through it, God's immense love for us is depicted by a heart with a cross going through it. It was painful for God to love us as much as He did. It will not necessarily be unpainful for Him to make us whole and real.

❋ ───────────────────────────

*Help me to be willing to accept the pain of being really loved by You.*

❋

*For he gives us comfort in our trials so that
we in turn may be able to give the same sort of
strong sympathy to others in theirs.*
*II Corinthians 1:4 (Phillips)*

Sometimes unanswered questions and
unsolvable problems can be the beginning of a
much deeper faith experience. At times like this
we are called to incorrigible faith and to receive
all that God wants to give us.

The apostle Paul reminds us that the grief
and pain from our unsolvable problems can have
a purpose, can give us an authentic faith to
share with others who are going through similar
trials. God wants to take the scars and wounds
in our lives and translate them through His
grace into a means of comfort and healing in
the lives of others.

❋ _____

*Take my wounds and my scars. Use them, Lord,
to bring Your healing to others.*

❋

*Though you have made me see troubles,*
*many and bitter, you will restore my life again;*
*from the depths of the earth you will again*
*bring me up. Psalm 71:20*

Our thin porcelain shell of pride insists
that we are too spiritually and socially mature to
have to engage in something so mundane as
loneliness. Hence, its subtle invasion in our lives
can be read on our faces, and in our whole posture even if we refuse to let the word cross our
lips.

Little do we realize that our quest for peace
must go through the loneliness. All of us will
have our own paths. Some are just longer than
others. Some wider. Some with more stones and
obstacles. But not to walk the path is to get lost.

❋ ────────────────────────────

*Father, I walk the path, through loneliness,*
*to Your peace and restoration.*

❧

*Praise be to the Lord, to God our Savior, who daily bears our burdens. Psalm 68:19*

Just the other night a lady said to me, "How do you do it?"

And I had to respond, "I don't. I am fighting for my very dignity right now. I'm struggling just to keep the boat upright."

The tears in her eyes gave evidence that hearing this was probably what she needed—not hearing how somebody has whipped the pain and conquered it totally.

You and I are simply fellow strugglers. None of us has our life or our pain completely in control, although we sometimes try to pretend that we do.

❧ _____

*Lord, You know my burdens are too heavy
for me to bear. I'm counting on You.*

❈

*For as he thinketh in his heart, so is he.*
*Proverbs 23:7a (KJV)*

The mind and the body are one. What you do physically will affect you mentally and emotionally. We've heard that so many times it has lost its power. We can lie to ourselves, and even to God, but we cannot lie to our bodies. Our bodies will always end up telling the truth about our repressed feelings.

One of the best things we can do amidst difficult feelings is strenuous exercise. Stretch your body. Stretch your emotions. Stretch your spirit. Stretch your mind. The greatest releasers of emotions are prayer and exercise. They are God's design to help us let go of frustration.

❈ ───────────────────────────

*Integrate my body, soul, and spirit, God,*
*and teach me how to stretch.*

*How long, O Lord? Will you forget me forever? How long will you hide your face from me? How long must I wrestle with my thoughts and every day have sorrow in my heart? Psalm 13:1, 2a*

Someone once told us "don't think with your feelings." That's good advice. But what many of us heard was "don't feel your feelings." We heard "it's not okay to get upset, to feel lonely, to get frustrated, to feel emotional pain." What we don't realize is that by repressing these painful feelings, we put a lid on positive feelings as well. It's no wonder we struggle to feel all the love and joy and peace that we would like to feel.

We serve a God of great feelings, great passion; you can't miss that in Scripture. The same God who listened to Job's agony, to Jonah's wailing, to Elijah's depression, and to the psalmist's pain and struggles is ready to listen to us.

---

*Hear my frustration, Lord. Hear the pain that I've been carrying from one day to the next.*

❀

*Sing to the Lord, you saints of his; praise his
holy name. For his anger lasts only a moment,
but his favor lasts a lifetime; weeping may
remain for a night, but rejoicing comes in
the morning. Psalm 30:4, 5*

Feelings are a source of energy. Feelings are
messages. They help us know who and where
we are. When we lose touch with our feelings,
we lose touch with that which makes us
human.

To deny your feelings is to deny a great portion of yourself. It's very hard, if not impossible,
to be real if you're repressing the emotional side
of your being. We were made in the image of
God—and that includes a whole spectrum of
feelings.

❀ _____

*How I thank You, God, that You created me with
feelings. Help me to listen to them and learn.*

❧

*Today, when you hear his voice, do not harden your hearts as in the rebellion, on the day of testing in the wilderness, where your fathers put me to the test and saw my works for forty years.*
*Hebrews 3:7b–9 (RSV)*

In the wilderness you experience life first-hand. If you don't fix dinner, you don't eat. If you don't put up the shelter, you get wet.

Like the Israelites at the time of the Exodus, in our inner wilderness we are stripped of our normal conveniences and asked to make a journey into the unknown. The wilderness—exterior or interior—is always a time of radical dependence upon God. When the going got tough for God's chosen people, they complained that they would rather be back under the control of the Egyptians. But their wilderness experience was never intended to be an end in itself, it was a time of preparation for a promise.

❧ ——————————————

*God, You are my only hope. Keep me going through the wilderness of my life, anticipating the fulfillment of Your promise.*

❀

*But I the Lord will answer them; I, the God of
Israel, will not forsake them. I will make rivers
flow on barren heights, and springs within the
valleys. I will turn the desert into pools of water,
and the parched ground into springs.*
*Isaiah 41:17b, 18*

If our lives were only sunshine, they would
be a desert. We are called to a firm meaning in
spite of all the tragedies about us and within us.
God wants to create a garden in our wilderness,
an oasis where we can again be refreshed.

Still we sometimes choose to numb ourselves
to the pain, to be distracted, to put on insulation, to seek escapes. But if we are to discover
the depth of solitude in the heart of loneliness,
we cannot continually go around the pain. To
the best of our abilities we must wade through
the emotions that we experience, no matter
what the cost. Our God will use these painful
times to draw us into deeper intimacy with
Him.

❀ ————————————————————

*Create a garden in the desert places of
my heart, God.*

❧

*I am in pain and distress; may your salvation,*
*O God, protect me. Psalm 69:29*

C.S. Lewis said that God whispers to us in our joys, speaks to us in our conscience, and shouts to us in our pain. In our joys, it is as though He is whispering in a crowded auditorium of His immense, outrageous love for us—but we can't hear. We're too busy. We're too enmeshed with our lives.

He tries again to speak to us through our conscience, but we don't slow down enough to listen. Our hearing aid is on low because we're engaged with so many things. Without purposeful listening the communication process is not complete.

But the Hound of heaven is persistent in His love and concern, so He shouts . . . through pain. He finally has our attention.

❧ ──────────────────────────

*Hound of heaven, You have my attention.*
*Help me to hear and understand.*

❧

*Every day I will praise you and extol your name*
*for ever and ever. Psalm 145:2*

None of us knows exactly what we will find in our own inner wilderness. There will be difficult places as well as awesome beauty. There will be hard grinds and oases. There will be moving experiences, and some experiences we would like to avoid altogether.

But the more time we spend in the wilderness, the more comfortable we become there. The rugged terrain turns into veritable adventure. The unique beauty is an invitation to the mystery of living, and we begin to appreciate the gift of each day.

❧ ─────────────────────────

*Because You are there in the middle of my wilderness, I can bear the pain and discover the beauty.*

❖

*I spread out my hands to you; my soul thirsts for you like a parched land. Psalm 143:6*

When it comes to the wilderness of the heart, I must expect the unexpected. The dark feelings have something to teach me which I can learn no other way. I must open up to all that God wants to teach me. There are experiences that He wants to give me so I can learn. Nobody else can experience it for me, nor can I experience it if I keep pushing it away by distraction and detour.

The only way out is through. If God is going to make His imprint in our lives, we must be willing to go through our feelings—not to let them dictate to us, but just to experience them.

❖ ————————————————————————

*Help me walk through my own wilderness, Father. Make Your lasting imprint on my life.*

❧

*In my inner being I delight in God's law, but I see another law at work in the members of my body, waging war against the law of my mind and making me a prisoner of the law of sin at work within my members. What a wretched man I am! Who will rescue me from this body of death? Romans 7:22–24*

I have found that I can enjoy the inner wilderness. Feeling new feelings, taking a chance, not playing it safe, getting in touch with more of me. I don't need to avoid the painful experiences in my life. It requires going behind the words to the music, even if it is a little off-key. It means experiencing God. Making real contact. Letting my heart be thrashed and rearranged if necessary.

> *There is no shortcut to wholeness: If you want to reach the Promised Land you must first go through the wilderness.*
> CLIFTON BURKE

❧ ───────────────────────────

*Lord, I want to be whole. Help me to face boldly the temptations and pains of life, knowing that through them I can experience You.*

⚜

*No, I beat my body and make it my slave so that after I have preached to others, I myself will not be disqualified for the prize. I Corinthians 9:27*

Some people, while going through difficult emotions, have taken their time of struggle as an opportunity to improve their physical fitness—and in doing so they impacted their emotional state in a positive way. So go ahead: get physical with your emotions. Use the large muscles of your body; do aerobics, cycle, run, walk! The more frustrated you are by your feelings, the more you need to stretch yourself physically.

Treat yourself to a new pair of running shorts—the brighter the better. Move. Take charge. Don't just sit back and wait for an answer. Make something happen today. Do five minutes of exercise. It all begins with a tiny step.

⚜ ————————————————————————

*Lord, thank You for the practical resources You have provided to handle emotional pain.*

❧

*Surely you desire truth in the inner parts, you*
*teach me wisdom in the inmost place.*
**Psalm 51:6**

Like me, you may have learned to dress up
your unacceptable feelings to make them look
good. You may be able to disguise them so clev-
erly that sometimes you don't even realize they
are only imitation feelings. They are nice, bland,
antiseptic, thimble–size feelings that are okay for
a church picnic but inadequate for a relationship
of any depth, even with yourself—and especially
with God.

If we do not "ex–press" our real feelings they
will come out in some way through our bodies—tense muscles, headaches, backaches,
depression, fatigue, or various other symptoms.

We can learn how to wade through the
wilderness of our emotions, no matter how
painful. It requires a difficult and deeper kind of
courage—but what an adventure!

❧ _____

*Give me courage, God, to wade through the difficult*
*wilderness of my conflicting emotions.*

***All my longings lie open before you, O Lord; my sighing is not hidden from you. Psalm 38:9***

Anne was raised in a home where expression of real feelings was taboo. She could smile and be content, but to be excessive in her joy was not acceptable. Likewise anger was not ladylike, and loneliness meant you weren't letting God love you. She was supposed to be a "good girl"—obedient, submissive, and thoughtful.

Now in her forties, Anne says, "There is a whole washing machine full of feelings going on inside of me, and I can't sort them out. I feel like I'm going to explode."

Therapist David Norton says, "I marvel at how we so value our spiritual and cognitive aspects while devaluing the emotional—as if God, when He was creating us, only got two-thirds of it right. Jesus died to take away our sins, not our feelings."

---

*Father God, I am grateful that, even though my emotions are sometimes an enigma to me, You understand them, every one.*

❁

*. . . there was given me a thorn in my flesh, a messenger of Satan, to torment me. Three times I pleaded with the Lord to take it away from me. But he said to me, "My grace is sufficient for you, for my power is made perfect in weakness." II Corinthians 12:7b–9a*

For years, people have asked me, "Haven't you prayed for healing?"

My obvious answer: "Of course."

"Why do you think God hasn't healed you?"

"He has."

"But I thought you were still in pain."

"I am. I have prayed hundreds of times for the Lord to heal me—and He finally *healed me of the need to be healed.*" I finally realized that if the Lord could use this body better the way it is, then that's the way it should be. For the past several years, I've had the opportunity to be on the steepest learning curve of my life. I'm quite sure I would be a different person, were it not for my accident.

❁ _____

*How could I live for You, Jesus, if You did not turn my weakness into strength?*

*That is why, for Christ's sake, I delight
in weaknesses, in insults, in hardships, in
persecutions, in difficulties. For when I am
weak, then I am strong. II Corinthians 12:9, 10*

As I learn new levels of giving over my situation to the Lord, I realize that it not only lessens my pain but increases my ability to be joyful in the midst of the circumstances.

Despite our inability to control circumstances, we have the gift of being free to respond to our situation in our own way, creatively or destructively. The more we fight our pain and sorrow, the more tense we become and the more the pain is amplified. When we stop grasping for immediate solutions, relax into the present moment, and even lean into the pain, we allow God to use the situation to transform us into the image of His Son.

*Help me lean into the pain of my situation,
Lord, and free me to grow in Your image.*

❧

*However, as it is written: "No eye has seen, no ear has heard, no mind has conceived what God has prepared for those who love him"—but God has revealed it to us by his Spirit.*
*I Corinthians 2:9, 10*

Victor Frankl, in his classic *Man's Search for Meaning*, shares the tragedies that he had to go through when thrown into a Nazi concentration camp. He lost his friends, his life work, the manuscripts he was working on, and even his family, but not his choice of attitude.

This became a significant turning point in his life, and it was from this discovery that he developed the concept of logo therapy—in essence the ability to find meaning through every event in life, even those most difficult.

Pain and suffering can force us to discover life on a deeper and more meaningful level.

❧ _____

*It's so easy to be superficial about life, Father. But through my pain, You help me discover the deeper levels.*

❖

*The grace of the Lord Jesus be with God's
people. Amen. Revelation 22:21*

GRACE. Perhaps no one ever completely
understands it. Few of us wholly recognize the
work of grace in our lives—yet God wants
more than anything for us to experience it with
as much fullness as we can handle.

Why do we miss it? First, we get stuck in the
surface of life. We get caught up with doing, to
the exclusion of the being element of our faith.

Second, our insistence on self–sufficiency—an
apparently harmless tendency—detours us from
a greater sense of completeness than we would
ever imagine.

Third, we avoid pain, which inadvertently
closes the door to the life in grace that we are
seeking at the deepest levels. Our fear of pain
blocks our ability to hear God in the depths of
our being.

❖ ———————————————————

*Lord Jesus, Your grace sustains me and enables
me to face the pain head on.*

❋

*Although he was a son, he learned obedience from what he suffered and, once made perfect, he became the source of eternal salvation for all who obey him. Hebrews 5:8, 9*

An advantage of disadvantages is that we have the opportunity to be transformed by our suffering. To be pushed. Pulled. Moved in one direction or another. Pain and suffering produce a fork in the road. It is not possible to remain unchanged. To let others or circumstances dictate your future is to have chosen. To allow the pain to corrode your spirit is to have chosen. And to be transformed into the image of Christ by these difficult and trying circumstances is to have chosen.

Even the Master had to go through suffering to learn obedience. Why should it be any less necessary for us?

❋ ─────────────────────────────

*Lord, I choose to take the road that will turn my suffering into Your agent for change.*

*But we have this treasure in jars of clay to show that this all–surpassing power is from God and not from us. II Corinthians 4:7*

Many of us try to get out of pain as fast as we can, so we can be more "useful" to God. Yet God reminds us again and again throughout Scripture that His greatest treasure fills earthen vessels in order to show that the transcendent power belongs to God and not to us, that in our weakness, we are strong.

Earthen vessels are God's first choice. Let God fill you just as you are. Let Him touch you and use you in your fragile and fallible state.

*Touch this cracked earthen vessel with Your power, God, and use me for Your glory.*

❧

*You need to persevere so that when you have done the will of God, you will receive what he has promised. . . . "But my righteous one will live by faith. And if he shrinks back, I will not be pleased with him." Hebrews 10:36, 38*

Pain and suffering can either be a prison or a prism. The tests of life are not to break us but to make us. We're called not to flinch from real trouble, for the greater part of life occurs in the inner man.

At the end of Paul's letter to the Galatians he talks about the scars he carries on his body because of his faith. Paul had an eyeball–to–eyeball experience with the risen Christ and discovered that the freedom he was called to was not painless, easy, nor without difficulty. But it was real.

❧ _____

*Give me courage to embrace the pain and suffering of life and be set free to experience You in a new way, Oh Risen Christ.*

# CHOOSE LIFE

❀

*Our gospel came to you not simply with words,*
*but also with power, with the Holy Spirit and*
*with deep conviction. I Thessalonians 1:5a*

Within each of us lies the capacity to be happy—to enjoy life and to change our attitude when we can't change the circumstances. Through the power of the Holy Spirit we can transcend the situation and create an inner environment that supersedes the external one. As Victor Frankl concluded after his experience in a Nazi concentration camp, "They could take everything from me except one thing—and that was the attitude with which I chose to respond to the situation."

❀ _____

*You have given me a choice, Lord, and through the*
*power of the Holy Spirit I choose life.*

*His divine power has bestowed on us everything that makes for life and true religion, enabling us to know the One who called us by his own splendor and might. II Peter 1:3 (NEB)*

All the discipline in the world cannot make the sun rise any earlier, or a flower more fragrant, or a smile more spontaneous. Running five miles a day will add as much as a hundred miles of capillaries to your system, make you feel more alive, but it won't necessarily teach you how to laugh. You don't have to have a plan to clap your hands. As someone once said, "If you have to move even ten inches from where you are now in order to be happy, then you will never be truly happy."

Can you imagine the sadness of seeing someone squinting at the horizon desperately, while what he is looking for is right at his feet?

*Help me to see the graces of life in my own backyard.*

❀

*Redeeming the time, because the days are evil.*
*Ephesians 5:16 (KJV)*

For a Christian there is no such thing as "free time." All of the Christian's time is redeemed and belongs to the One who has set us free. Therefore, it is impossible for a committed believer to say his working time is more valuable than his leisure time.

In leisure the mind is liberated from the immediate, the usual, the necessary problems, to meditate on ultimate matters. Through leisure we are given permission to develop a new perspective on life. Through leisure we may come to better understand the wonder of being alive and to take time to share it with those we love.

❀ ————————————————————

*Thank You that You call me to leisure*
*as well as to work.*

*I tell you the truth, anyone who will not receive the kingdom of God like a little child will never enter it. Luke 18:17*

God can teach us many things through children. Laughter doesn't have to be taught to children. Play doesn't have to be justified. Rest is a natural part of their life–style. Every day I realize more and more that we have something to learn from these little encyclopedias of life.

They can teach us of wonder and uninhibitedness, of gratitude and spontaneity, of unimpeded trust and freedom to change, of imagination and creativity. They can teach us to see things as if it were for the first time and to share as if there were no end. They can teach us how to smell again, and taste, and touch. And they can teach us why God calls us to be like little children.

*God, open my senses to the wonder of life, as though I were once again a child.*

❀

*Later, Jesus spoke to the people again and said: "I am the light of the world. The man who follows me will never walk in the dark but will live his life in the light." John 8:12 (Phillips)*

Leisure is more than just nonwork. It is a point of contact with reality and a catalyst for new experiences, new ideas, new people, and new places. It is the time when the gift of wholeness again becomes a hope and a possibility.

Prayer, *recreatio mentis in Deum* ("the recreation of the soul in God"), is necessarily an act of leisure. Play, when our spirits finally respond to Jesus' command to be more childlike, is an expression of not only the value of leisure, but of life itself.

More today than ever, we need to learn how to give ourselves permission to relax, to play, to enjoy life, and to enjoy God for who He is.

❀ ——————————————————————

*Thank You, God, for the gift of leisure, of play, of the times when You can pull me aside into Your light.*

*For ye are bought with a price: therefore glorify God in your body, and in your spirit, which are God's. I Corinthians 6:20 (KJV)*

The essential purpose of being alive is to know God, glorify Him, and enjoy Him forever.

What does this mean in daily life? The first thing we need to recognize is that we live in an amphibian world of both work and leisure. To look at one without the other is blindness. They are complimentary. We must challenge some of our superficial views of work.

If we do, the result will be not only a deeper understanding of both work and leisure, but also a reconciliation of the two in our own lifestyles. And God will invade our lives at a level more profound than we've experienced before.

*May my daily life glorify You, Father, in a healthy balance of work and leisure.*

❧

*The heavens declare the glory of God; the skies proclaim the work of his hands. Day after day they pour forth speech; night after night they display knowledge. Psalm 19:1, 2*

We can get to the place where we no longer savor life for what it is. We bolt down our life as if it were a hamburger patty getting cold on the edge of a shivering plate. We insatiably gulp down our incomplete and undigested experiences as fast as we can stuff them in— as if there were no tomorrow.

Each tired day covers us with another layer of insulation—the noise, the clutter, the crowds, the busyness—our awareness grows so dim and superficial that nothing seems so lonely to us as our simple being. We no longer savor life for what it is.

Life is a miracle. Life is an instant. A glimpse. A gift!

❧ ─────────────────────────────

*Forgive me, Lord, for the busyness that has crowded out the wonder of life.*

*I will praise you, O Lord, with all my heart;
I will tell of all your wonders. Psalm 9:1*

Being creative means taking everyday material and turning it into something extraordinary. Each of us is unique, formed in the image of the Creator. That means that each of us has the gift of creativity, but to fully explore our creativity takes commitment, hard work, and enthusiasm. Interestingly, the word "enthusiasm" comes from a Greek root meaning "God within you." Therefore since God is within us, we all have sufficient enthusiasm to complete any project—all we have to do is express that enthusiasm.

Light filters through the window from its source some 93 million miles away. We are surrounded by the many miracles of life, and our world is as vast as our imaginations—or as small. The choice is ours.

*Creator God, God within me, open my
eyes to the miracles of life.*

❧

*I love you, O Lord, my strength. . . . In my distress I called to the Lord; I cried to my God for help. From his temple he heard my voice; my cry came before him, into his ears. Psalm 18:1, 6*

Emotions are a gift from God, given to us so we can respond to life.

My Bible is crammed and overflowing with a passionate God who seeks out His people—men and women who loved Him passionately in return.

My Bible says that David was a man of great emotion, that Mary Magdalene loved Jesus with all her heart, that Moses thundered with passion in all he did, that Paul caused a fervor on more than one occasion, that Peter didn't make little mistakes—and that God loves His people with great passion.

❧ _____

*As I think of the strength of David's love for You—of Mary Magdalene's—I am embarrassed for the puny passion of my devotion. Forgive me.*

❧

*I have never stopped thanking God for you. I pray for you constantly, asking God, the glorious Father of our Lord Jesus Christ, to give you wisdom to see clearly and really understand who Christ is and all that he has done for you.*
*Ephesians 1:16, 17 (TLB)*

We have become a mass of isolated people, perplexed and hardened. We have more sophisticated techniques than ever before in history, but no communication—no connection. Like cars caught in rush-hour traffic, we seem lost, weaving from one lane to the next, struggling to get home.

The odometer on our lives keeps turning over. We need not repair, not a mere tune-up, but restoration. Transformation. We need more than just to fill our tanks. We need to discover a cup that ever overflows. We need more than just our windshields cleaned—we need new eyes.

❧ _____

*I need restoration, Lord. Transformation. Open my eyes to understand anew who You really are.*

❋

*No matter what happens, always be thankful, for this is God's will for you who belong to Christ Jesus. I Thessalonians 5:18 (TLB)*

Sometimes life is not so much to be understood as it is to be lived out. Some of us spend more time analyzing life than we do living it. I need to remind you that joy is another way in which we express our gratitude for the one who lives within us and allow Him to be expressed into a world that needs so many things—especially our grateful joy.

I encourage you to both say and experience the words *Hallelujah . . . anyway*! Even if it's Monday. Even if it's six–thirty in the morning. Even if your washer ate the socks for the third time this week. Even if your car died the week after your warranty expired. Even if your vacations are only fifteen minutes long these days.

❋ ————————————————————————

*Oh Father, sometimes I can't sincerely thank You for my circumstances, but I can be joyfully grateful for Your presence in those circumstances.*

❄

*Do not put out the Spirit's fire.*
*I Thessalonians 5:19*

Christianity does not consist in abstaining from doing things no gentleman would think of doing," says R. L. Sheppard, "but in doing things that are unlikely to occur to anyone who is not in touch with the Spirit of Christ."

We have the power to convert any situation into a mission of gladness.

The mother of some friends of mine who was still vibrant in her eighties, was standing in a rather lengthy line waiting for tickets. The line hadn't moved and the rain wouldn't stop. Rather than be dismal, she asked someone to save her place in line for a few moments. A short time later she returned with thirty doughnuts, which she proceeded to give away to cheer everybody up. She had converted a rather dull moment into a magic one.

❄ ———————————————————————

*I want to be open to Your Spirit to see those*
*opportunities for "missions of gladness."*

❀

*Let us hold unswervingly to the hope we profess, for he who promised is faithful. And let us consider how we may spur one another on toward love and good deeds. Hebrews 10:23, 24*

Have you ever walked all night under a full moon because you didn't reach your destination by sunset, and then found yourself singing in spite of your weariness because you were with some friends who felt like you did? Can you recall the last time you felt unique, fully alive, and like you were reaching for all your potential with all you had within you?

Have you ever wondered what the boundaries are for your physical, mental, or spiritual potential?

Historically God's people have been uninhibited risk takers, unafraid to dive right into the heart of life. Let the herd graze where it pleases. Put a little pepper on your Kentucky Fried Seagull and take a chance.

❀ ─────────────────────────────

*Lord, the possibilities are endless for diving into the heart of life! Where shall I start?*

❦

*I praise you because I am fearfully and wonderfully made; your works are wonderful, I know that full well. Psalm 139:14*

Play is more than just nonwork. Play reminds me I am a body—fearfully and wondrously made. I know from my reading that I have approximately 263 bones and 600 muscles, that I am a microcosm of the universe, containing 92 elements of the cosmos in my body. But play tells me that I am a living miracle, that I am not ordinary, that I am by creation more marvelous than all the statistics ever compiled and categorized. As George Sheehan points out, "There are those who, like Freud, claim that the two main goals in life are love and work. What they fail to see is the primacy of play. Before love, before work, there was play. . . . Play is a taste of the Paradise from which we came, a foretaste of the Paradise we will enter."

❦ ————————————————————

*Surely Your great love is also seen in the way play re—creates my whole person. Thank You, Lord.*

❦

*He seldom reflects on the days of his life, because*
*God keeps him occupied with gladness of heart.*
*Ecclesiastes 5:20*

One of the most important principles of quality leisure is focusing on what we have rather than on what we don't. It is the absence of comparison between me and you, rich and poor, life and death, work and play.

Is it so small a thing to enjoy our days and to enjoy God and to enjoy being who we are? Is it so small a thing to be grateful and to be happy, to be at peace with ourselves and with God? Is it so small a thing to fly a kite with your child, to take a walk, to play catch, to wrestle on the lawn, to tickle and be tickled until your laughter can't be controlled? Is it so small a thing to make our days count rather than count our days?

❦ _____

*Oh God, remind me today of the "small things,"*
*and help me to make this day count.*

✲

*Once you were not a people, but now you are the people of God; once you had not received mercy, but now you have received mercy. I Peter 2:10*

The media, especially advertisers, have two consistent and dominant messages. The first is that "you are not OK!" Every manufacturer must persuade you that you are not yet complete, that you lack something you need to be happy, i.e., their product. The second message is that you must never be satisfied—products cannot be just different; one must be superior.

Sometimes I have the feeling that my life has not yet started, and I'm still waiting for the proper moment to begin. Yet unless we live fully in the present, the future will always be a disappointment. Each day is a new, unrepeatable, once–in–a–lifetime gift. To waste it by always waiting for tomorrow, by thinking that enough is never enough, is pure folly.

✲ ─────────────────────────────

*You have given me all I need for right now— for this moment. Thank You.*

❈

*Since my youth, O God, you have taught me,*
*and to this day I declare your marvelous deeds.*
*Psalm 71:17*

We all long for certainty, the answers to
our many questions. But the life of faith implies
living the questions, wandering through our
fears and hopes, and somehow shuffling our way
with tenacity and courage toward Bethlehem.
Robert Raines says that "The Bible is a book of
journeys and questions—of people asking God
questions and God questioning His people."

We must live out the questions with gladness
and hunger. The process of living life is long,
arduous, complex, and certainly not painless—
but it's worth it. And we need not wait until the
conclusion to celebrate. We can, if we choose,
celebrate the process.

❈ _____

*Lord, I don't have many answers, but in faith I look*
*to You to guide me through the questions.*

*So then, men ought to regard us as servants of Christ and as those entrusted with the secret things of God. I Corinthians 4:1, 2*

On one of our Summit Expedition Wilderness courses for adults, we had the privilege of having Dr. Carver of Point Loma Nazarene College as speaker. One moment, when just he and I were talking, he said something I'll never forget.

"In recent years, I've learned three things that have changed how I view my life. The first is that my primary opportunity and obligation in life is to be a Christian—not a department head or any of the many roles I play.

"The second thing is that I don't know what that actually means. I am called, as Paul says, to be a steward of the mystery of Christ.

"And third, because of this I am forced to my knees each day to discover by grace what it means and how to live it out."

*Lord, I need a generous supply of Your grace to understand and carry out Your mission for my life.*

❧

*For I wrote you out of great distress and anguish
of heart and with many tears, not to grieve you
but to let you know the depth of my love for you.*
***II Corinthians 2:4***

Feelings are simply our responses to information, truth, and experience. And when we simply learn to feel our feelings—to identify them clearly and express them accurately—we not only can stop negative patterns but feel the power of joy that is our promise.

Our Christian walk is made up of at least three parts: fact, faith, and feelings. These are like a three–legged stool. If you pull one leg away, the stool will fall over. Feelings are a part of any love relationship, even our relationship with God. Feelings are what keep the relationship alive. We must know God with our heart as well as with our head.

❧ _____

*Thank You for the freedom to feel both the
negative and positive vibrations of life.*

*Then you will know the truth, and the truth will set you free. John 8:32*

The longer I live the more appreciative I become of the fact that life is not tidy and predictable. But it is filled with all the emotions that we can handle—and sometimes even more. I'm grateful that we never know who we will become—and that's why it's called a journey.

I am learning that there is a center within all of us where truth abides in fullness—and that it can be discovered and, even more importantly, it can be experienced. I'm learning that it's worth all the pain to find it. And that wherever possible, we're meant to share it. I am learning that each moment of life is in itself a sacred privilege. Life's moments are complete in themselves. Part of the joy is discovering that; the better part is participating in it.

*I look to You, Jesus, to take my hand and guide me on this wonderful journey to truth and freedom.*

❦

*Being confident of this, that he who began a good
work in you will carry it on to completion until
the day of Christ Jesus. Philippians 1:6*

William Stafford was once asked, "When
did you decide to become a poet?" He responded, "Everyone is born a poet—a person discovering the way words sound and work, caring
and delighting in words. I just kept on doing
what everyone starts out doing."

We all need to discover and keep rediscover-
ing the poetry of our own existence. All of our
lives are like patchwork quilts. How dull and
dreary they would be without darker patches to
contrast with the lighter ones. Many of us have
never realized how dreary and lifeless our existence would be without problems and difficulties. Part of the blessing of the human journey is
that we are, in fact, human, and therefore wonderfully complex and changing constantly.

❦ ———————————————————————

*Thank You, Father, that You are with me all
through this exciting, complex journey.*

# Choose Life!

❧

***I have chosen the way of truth.***
***Psalm 119:30a***

Paul Tournier says that perhaps the most powerful and unused gift from God is choice. For me a big step in maturity was letting go of the fantasy of some magical cure and beginning to understand that pain can either integrate or disintegrate me. The choice is up to me.

Pain is teaching me how to choose more forcefully, more boldly. I'm learning how to say no with more aggressiveness, sometimes because I simply have to. I'm learning how to say yes with more honesty and openness because my life has become more vulnerable.

The root of the word *decide* means "to cut." Perhaps one of the advantages of disadvantages is the fact that we have to cut. We have to make choices which we didn't have to at earlier stages in our life.

❧ _____

*Choices are difficult, God. I need Your help to make certain choices with honesty and openness.*

❀

*Many, O Lord my God, are the wonders you have done. The things you planned for us no one can recount to you; were I to speak and tell of them, they would be too many to declare.*
*Psalm 40:5*

On a day when my pain level was almost intolerable I visited with Joni Eareckson Tada, the gifted author/artist/singer who has been a quadriplegic since a diving accident at age seventeen. When I got home I collapsed at the kitchen table and indulged in a bout of self–pity. Suddenly my younger son, Joshua, came running into the room and jumped into my arms. As I hugged him, I had an embarrassed realization: Joni, who had been so buoyant and cheerful all day, would never be able to experience giving such a hug. Perhaps for the first time in my life, I realized that being able to give my son a hug was a gift and not a right, and even the simplest acts and events are meant to be treasured.

❀ _____

*How often I take the simple pleasures of life for granted, Lord.*

✿

*Therefore, since we have been justified through faith, we have peace with God through our Lord Jesus Christ, through whom we have gained access by faith into this grace in which we now stand. And we rejoice in the hope of the glory of God. Romans 5:1, 2*

I think of Howard Butt's profoundly simple question: "Which would you rather have—a Christian reputation or Jesus Christ?" and know again that it is not vital for me to appear to others to be a "victorious Christian." If my pain has taught me anything, it is to be who I am in Christ, without images or pretense. I am slowly learning what it means to be free in Christ.

Being justified in Christ means, among other things, that I don't have to keep continually justifying myself. I am slowly discovering a radical (in the sense of its etymology, "rooted") kind of self–acceptance—because of and in spite of my limitations.

Truth is free, but not easy.

✿ ———————————————————————

*I'm thankful that I can be what I really am with You, Jesus. No pretense. What freedom!*

❦

*Let the peace of Christ rule in your hearts, since as members of one body you were called to peace. And be thankful. Colossians 3:15*

There came a time in my life when the pace I was trying to maintain had no time for rhythm and awe, for mystery and wonder. In order to keep up my incessant activity, God was simply reduced to fit into my schedule.

I realized that if I wanted to be truly, radically committed to Jesus Christ, I would have to stop doing at least some of what I was doing.

When you come to such a spiritual intersection, you may have to choose between apparent "success"—living up to someone else's standards—or true contentment in your own uniqueness, based on a deep self–acceptance imbedded in the unconditional love of Christ. It is then that you realize: What you are is more important than what you do.

❦ _____

*If I were honest with You, Lord, I would admit that I'm tired of all the "doing." Teach me how to "be."*

*On the third day there was a wedding at
Cana–in–Galilee. The mother of Jesus was there
and Jesus and his disciples were guests also.
John 2:1, 2 (NEB)*

The "Bionic Christian" is the super
Christian who is, at least in appearance, above
reproach. He has been redeemed, even of his
humanness, and he works hard daily to earn
righteousness. Each of his answers is quick and
precise, and his time is managed with calculated
economy. Above all else, no time is wasted on
laughter and play when there is so much to be
done in the world. Heavily laden with guilt and
tension about each of the minutes he might be
wasting, the Bionic Christian simply does not
have time to be happy. Irony of ironies, his
commitment to Jesus Christ has become a
prison rather than a blessing. He forgets that
Jesus, despite the sad world He inhabited, was
the prime host and the prime guest of the party.

*Cast away my need to be "righteous,"
Oh joyful Jesus, and bring me to the party.*

❀

*You are looking only on the surface of things.*
*II Corinthians 10:7a*

Pain forces you to look below the surface. But many of us never have the courage to choose to do that. Hence we waste much of our life in bitterness and complaint, always looking for something else, never realizing that perhaps God has already given us sufficient grace to discover all of what we are looking for in the midst of our circumstances.

St. Thomas Aquinas told of a man who heard about a very special ox and determined to have it for his own. He traveled all over the world. He spent his entire fortune. He gave his whole life to the search for this ox. At last, just moments before he died, he realized he had been riding it all the time.

❀ _____

*Forgive my complaining, Lord. Thank You for Your present and sufficient grace, available to me right now, right here.*

❈

*Is not life more important than food,
and the body more important than clothes?*
*Matthew 6:25b*

A few years ago I had a conversation with an elderly gentleman who radiated a strong and genuine serenity. Somewhere in our conversation he said, "As I get older, I seem to place less importance on material things." And then, after a pause, he continued, "Come to think of it, I place less importance on importance."

Society has inundated us with the importance of importance. We have been conditioned to believe in the big, the fast, the expensive, and the far away. I'm still convinced that if you have to move even ten inches from where you are now in order to be happy, you never will be. Life becomes precious and more special to us when we look for the little everyday miracles and get excited again about the privilege of simply being human.

❈ ─────────────────────

*It's so easy to be sidetracked by society's messages,
God. Today I celebrate the privilege of
simply being human.*

***Shout with joy to God, all the earth! Sing to the glory of his name; make his praise glorious!***
***Psalm 66:1, 2***

In our overemphasis on "important" things, we often overlook the intrinsic value of life itself. We have begun to believe the radio and TV commercials and have put so many overlays on our life that we can no longer see the fine–grained texture of everyday life.

Have we forgotten how special Wednesdays can be? Have we somehow fallen into the rut where all Mondays are dreary or February is a difficult month? Have we gotten trapped into comparisons and ingratitudes? Are we in the habit of always putting off an experience until we can afford it? Or until the time is right?

*"The truth is that life is delicious,*
*horrible, charming, sweet, bitter,*
*and that is everything."* ANATOLE FRANCE

Now is as good as any time to jump in.

---

*Thank You for life in all its flavors—bitter, delicious, sweet, bland. I will taste it all, and praise You with joy.*

❁

*But to each of us grace has been given as Christ apportioned it. Ephesians 4:7*

Grace is free, but it certainly isn't cheap. You may have read the story of David Rothenberg a few years ago. His father, in a fit of rage, went into David's room, poured kerosene all over the room and all over the tiny boy, and lit him on fire. In God's difficult grace, David somehow lived through it, though ninety-five percent of his body was covered with third—degree burns. It is estimated that David will have approximately 5,000 operations in his lifetime. Each year they have to open him up so that he can grow. Along with a few saints and poets, David Rothenberg is aware of the greatest miracle of all: LIFE ITSELF. At the age of 7, he had the audacity to say:

I am alive!
I am alive!
I am alive!
I didn't miss out on living! and that is wonderful enough for me.

❁ _____

*O Giver of life, how often I take
Your gift for granted.*

❧

*But because of his great love for us, God, who is*
*rich in mercy, made us alive with Christ even*
*when we were dead in transgressions.*
*Ephesians 2:4, 5a*

Perhaps the most important thing I have learned in my journey with pain is the intrinsic value of life itself—the sacredness of each unrepeatable moment. To partake of it is sheer gift; none of us did anything to deserve it. The most tangible form of grace itself is the substance of our normal everyday life. Perhaps it has been worth all the pain just to learn this one blessed lesson.

Helen Keller is one of my great heroines. Though struck deaf and blind at the age of two, she later said, "Life is either a daring adventure . . . or nothing at all."

❧ _____

*You are there, Christ Jesus, in the ordinary*
*moments, showering me with mercy, reminding*
*me of the wonder of life.*

*For you created my inmost being; you knit me together in my mother's womb. Psalm 139:13*

The human eye can see an estimated 8 *million* different colors. It's also estimated that 2 million signals are hitting our nervous system every second. We are Nature's greatest miracle. Our brain is capable of making and storing enough connections and information that the total number would be expressed by a one followed by 6.5 million miles of zeroes—a number that would stretch between the earth and moon and back fourteen times.

We could go on and on. "Fearfully and wonderfully made" begins to take on a whole new meaning. And our attitude of gratitude should be a little more acute, as, hopefully, we begin to realize what special beings we are and what special people we can become.

*Thank You, God, for the untapped wonders within me that You created for Your glory.*

❧

*I pray also that the eyes of your heart may be enlightened in order that you may know the hope to which he has called you, the riches of his glorious inheritance in the saints. Ephesians 1:18*

Paul Weber was one of our brightest and most talented Summit Expedition instructors. He was twenty–six, strong, an incredible athlete, vitally and vividly committed to Jesus Christ. He and his soon–to–be–wife planned to travel all over New Zealand and Australia on passes that he had saved while working at a travel agency. One evening we sat and talked together for four hours. A week later Paul died in a tragic accident.

Life is short—for some it's even shorter than it's "supposed" to be. Why such things happen is beyond me. But the question is, how can we, knowing that life is so delicious and short, continue to live bland, insipid lives . . . knowing that each day comes but once in human history?

❧ _____

*You have given me this present moment, Lord. Help me not to waste it.*

❋

*Do not boast about tomorrow, for you do not know what a day may bring forth. Proverbs 27:1*

I don't know how much string is left on my ball of twine. There are no guarantees as to how long any of us will live, but I know full well that I would rather make my days count than merely count my days. I want to live each one of them as close to the core of life as possible, experiencing as much of God and my family and friends as I am capable. Since life is inevitably too short for all of us, I know full well that I want to enjoy it as much as I can, no matter what the circumstances are.

❋ ───────────────────────────────────

*Help me to celebrate this day, this unrepeatable day, and not just count it.*

❧

*In my opinion whatever we may have to go
through now is less than nothing compared with
the magnificent future God has planned for us.
Romans 8:18 (Phillips)*

The voice on the other end of the phone
inquired with enthusiasm, "What does it mean for
a horse to be handicapped!?" It was Leigh, a special friend who suffers from severe cerebral palsy.

"Well, Leigh, they usually handicap the
strongest horse by adding a little extra weight to
make the race more fair."

"Yeah, I know! Then what does it mean if you
handicap a golfer?"

"The better the golfer, the larger the handicap."

"Yeah, I know. And what does it mean . . ." We
explored a number of sports with the same conclusion. There was a long pause.

"That's it!"

"That's what, Leigh?"

"That's it! That's why God gave me such a big
handicap . . . because I'm so special!"

❧ _____

*Sometimes I ask, "Why?" But You know
the answers, Lord. You see the magnificent future.*

❦

*You, my brothers, were called to be free.*
*Galatians 5:13a*

The big dream in our society is that if we work hard enough, we will eventually be able to experience a life without limitations or difficulties. It is also one of the sources of friction in our society, creating disappointment, unnecessary suffering, and missed opportunities to live a full life. Some people spend their entire life waiting for that which will and can never happen.

Limitations are not necessarily negative. In fact, I'm beginning to believe that they can give life definition, clarity, and freedom. We are called to a freedom of *and in* limitations—not from. Unrestricted water is a swamp—because it lacks restriction, it also lacks depth.

The conclusion we arrive at all depends upon how we look at our limitations.

❦ ――――――――――――――――――

*Beyond my limitations, God, You see freedom. Help me look at my limitations through Your eyes.*

❧

*For we who are alive are always being given over to death for Jesus' sake, so that his life may be revealed in our mortal body. II Corinthians 4:11*

I read the story of a young man who was a quadriplegic and yet affirmed life with an immense sense of joy. When asked what was his secret he said, "Even dressing is almost impossible for me. When life becomes this difficult, you know darn well I'm going to make sure that it's quality."

Many people live as though they regret God's incredible invitation to life. Avoiding pain becomes their chief occupation. And few of them realize that avoidance of difficulty only produces more pain in the long run.

The Bible is certainly not oblivious to difficulty. But it is critical that we begin to understand Scripture's message that difficulty and joy are not exclusive entities, but mutual friends.

❧ _____

*In the middle of my difficulties today, let me experience the joy of being alive in You.*

❦

*If my people would but listen to me . . . [they]*
*would be fed with the finest of wheat; with honey*
*from the rock I would satisfy . . .[them].*
*Psalm 81:13a, 16*

At the end of a college health course I
taught, I asked the class to tell me whose life
gave the concept of "wholeness" the most
meaning to them. They unanimously chose Tre
Bernhard, a member of the class. Some serious
congenital problems had left Tre with only one
leg that could do no more than hold a shoe. She
had a total of six stubby fingers. But Tre's two
most predominant features were her incredible
compassion and her lively sense of humor. Tre
had been through hardships even worse than
her physical handicaps, yet she chose to transcend the situation and give to the world a tangible sense of love and humor that changed
more than one life, including my own.

❦ ————————————————————

*Forgive me, Lord, for letting my minor difficulties*
*keep me from living my life in Your fullness.*

*O Lord, our Lord, how majestic is your name in all the earth! You have set your glory above the heavens. . . . When I consider your heavens, the work of your fingers, the moon and the stars, which you have set in place, what is man that you are mindful of him, the son of man that you care for him? Psalm 8:1, 3, 4*

Some people walk through life with gloves and a raincoat on, refusing to observe and experience the beauty and the wonder of the world around them. So many have forgotten the privilege of not only earthly delights, but also of our unearthly purpose. I see so many, including myself, who take our divine privilege for granted. Each day has its own distinctness and its own inexhaustibility. And yet how few realize it. Just because we take something for granted, doesn't mean it still isn't miraculous. Perhaps nothing is really ordinary.

*When I consider You and Your gifts, I am astonished by the miracles of life! Thank You.*

❧

*Every good and perfect gift is from above, coming down from the Father of the heavenly lights, who does not change like shifting shadows.*
*James 1:17*

Somewhere along the line I began to realize that the accident that had left me with life–long pain was more than just an interruption in my life, more than just a meddlesome interlude. It was a major intersection.

The crossroads forced a choice, and the choice was to give up or to live.

You and I are alive. It is a privilege that none of us can fully comprehend. It needn't have been so. The grace of everyday living is a gift.

Even in the midst of life's pain, there is no better time than the now. Open your eyes— otherwise the beauty will pass you by. Open your heart—else the truth will not walk with you.

❧ _____

*I don't want to miss the beauty of life, Father. My soul lifts in gratitude to You.*

# In Loneliness and Discouragement

❧❧

*Three times I was beaten with rods, once I was*
*stoned, three times I was shipwrecked, I spent a*
*night and a day in the open sea . . .*
*II Corinthians 11:25*

The Apostle Paul is sometimes referred to as
the greatest Christian who ever lived, but look at
what he encountered:

He received thirty-nine-lashes five times.

He was beaten three times with rods.

He was stoned.

He was shipwrecked three times.

All this occurred after he became a Christian.
Paul's writings indicate he tried to see the creative side of his stress and use his problems as
growing experiences for himself and others.

Like Paul, we may feel pressed on every side
by troubles, but we don't let them crush and
break us. We are often perplexed because we
don't know why things happen as they do, but
we don't give up and quit. We keep going
because we know God never abandons us.

❧❧ _____

*I cling to the promise, God, that*
*You will never abandon me.*

❧

*Then he said to them, "My soul is overwhelmed
with sorrow to the point of death. Stay here and
keep watch with me." Going a little farther, he
fell with his face to the ground and prayed, "My
Father, if it is possible, may this cup be taken
from me. Yet not as I will, but as you will."*
*Matthew 26:38, 39*

Even Jesus experienced loneliness. In
Gethsemane's garden He found His three closest
friends asleep. "Could you not watch with Me
for one hour?" He asked. He who was fully
God was fully human and knew the need for
human and divine companionship at the deepest
levels. Shortly after this incredibly lonely
moment, one of His disciples betrayed Him.

Yes, He fully understands our loneliness.
In fact, perhaps the loneliest statement ever
offered was Jesus' cry from the cross, "My God,
my God, why have you forsaken me?"
(Matthew 27:46).

❧ _____

*In my loneliness I look to You, Jesus,
for You know how loneliness feels.*

*I have hidden your word in my heart that I might not sin against you. . . . I meditate on your precepts and consider your ways. . . . I delight in your decrees; I will not neglect your word. Psalm 119:11, 15, 16*

There is a difference between memorizing Scripture and thinking biblically. There's a difference between knowing the words and experiencing their meaning. There is a difference between having the sentences embedded in your head and having their impact embedded in your heart. There is a difference between "doing Christianity" and being a Christian.

You can memorize all of the words, but if you've forgotten the music you still won't be able to sing the song. Most people say that we don't know enough Scripture. That's probably true. Paradoxically, however, we sometimes read it too much and experience it too little. Chuck Swindoll says we're called to read Scripture so deeply that our "blood runs Bibline."

*Renew my view of Your Word, God. Let it reach beyond my mind to my heart, my life.*

*Look at the birds of the air; they do not sow or reap or store away in barns, and yet your heavenly Father feeds them. Are you not much more valuable than they? Matthew 6:26*

We are a nation of people consumed by having. We want to have not only material things, but facts. We want to have knowledge. We want to have information. We even want to have love and inspiration. We want to have happiness and have abundance. Ownership seems to be the king of virtues, no matter what the commodity, and yet we are a society of notoriously unhappy people; lonely, anxious, depressed, dependent.

By now we should have learned that unrestricted satisfaction of all desires is not conducive to well-being. We know this to be true for our children, and yet sometimes we fail to recognize its truth in our own lives. Greed and peace preclude each other.

*I need Your grace, heavenly Father, to transform my need to "have."*

*As a result, it has become clear throughout the whole palace guard and to everyone else that I am in chains for Christ. Philippians 1:13*

I have heard it said that a person's life is based on what his thoughts are, what his basic attitude is about life. A pessimist sees a problem in every opportunity whereas an optimist sees an opportunity in every problem.

There comes a time—and it may well be the birth of maturity—when we come to realize that when we get through our present problems, there will probably be another one, perhaps slightly more difficult, waiting to take its place.

Most of the psalms were born in difficulty. Most of the epistles were written in prison. The critical difference in what is accomplished is attitude.

*Lord, I am confident that You can take whatever circumstance that greets me today and use it for Your purposes.*

***The Lord came and stood there, calling as at the
other times, "Samuel! Samuel!" Then Samuel
said, "Speak, for your servant is listening."
I Samuel 3:10***

Loneliness is not a time of abandonment.
It just feels that way. It's actually a time of
encounter at new levels with the only One who
can really heal that empty place in our hearts.

Loneliness is both a dying and a birth, a deep
pain and a threshold, a heartache and a thirst.

Although I know all too well the terrible
ache of loneliness, I also know that the wilderness of loneliness can be a place of great
adventure.

Lean into your loneliness. God is shouting to
you. Can you hear Him calling you by name?

*Is that Your voice I hear, God, calling me through
my loneliness and emptiness? Help me hear You.*

※

*But I trust in your unfailing love; my heart
rejoices in your salvation. I will sing to the Lord,
for he has been good to me. Psalm 13:5, 6*

Loneliness is feeling alone. Solitude is
being alone. Loneliness feels frantic. Solitude is
still and focused. Loneliness focuses on external
circumstances. Solitude focuses on the inner
adventure. Loneliness relies on what others
think and say about you. Solitude relies on what
God says about you and to you. Loneliness is a
reaction. Solitude is reflection. Loneliness focuses on absence and all you don't have. Solitude
focuses on presence and all God has given you.

※ ————————————————

*When I move through my loneliness to the quiet
place alone with You, I can sing again.*

❦

*How great is the love the Father has lavished on*
*us, that we should be called children of God!*
*I John 3:1a*

No one is immune to loneliness. I don't
care how long you have been a Christian, how
mature you are, how many people you have led
to the Lord. Loneliness is simply part of the
human predicament. It comes with love's territory. When you are truly lonely, simple cosmet-
ics don't work. You can't pretend that you're
okay.

Let God really love you. Make real contact.
Don't just tidy up. Let go. Light the fire. Bomb
the blockades to your heart.

The most dangerous journey is the journey
inward. Jesus bled real blood for each of us—
we've got to at least raise our pulse in return.

❦ ─────────────────────────────────

*Your lavish love washes over my soul, exposing the*
*hurt, making room for Your presence.*

*Therefore, as God's chosen people, holy and dearly loved, clothe yourselves with compassion, kindness, humility, gentleness and patience.*
*Colossians 3:12*

Have you heard this parable that illustrates the difference between heaven and hell? In both situations, people are sitting at a banquet table overflowing with bounteous food. In both scenarios, everyone seated at the table has splints strapped to their arms that cannot be removed.

In hell everyone is starving to death at the banquet table. But in heaven the banquet guests have discovered that since their arms are strapped, each person can feed the person across the table. Each feeds another, and all receive all they need.

Love is a celebration of giving as well as receiving. As we reach out in our brokenness, our arms splinted so that we cannot feed ourselves, we will be given what we need in return.

*Lord, You make it possible for my wounded spirit to bring Your touch to others.*

✣

*And now, brothers, we want you to know about the grace that God has given the Macedonian churches. Out of the most severe trial, their over-flowing joy and their extreme poverty welled up in rich generosity. II Corinthians 8:1, 2*

It has been said that no growth can occur until blaming ceases. As we cast our blame on others for their apparent lack of love, the ache will only grow deeper.

Some of us are looking so hard for the answer that we can't see the many gifts that surround us.

It is difficult to receive when your fists are clenched.

It is impossible to embrace when your arms are crossed.

It is difficult to see when your eyes are closed.

It is hard to discover when you mind is made up.

A heart sealed off from giving is sealed off from the ability to receive love.

✣ ───────────────────────────

*Unclench my fists, uncross my arms, and open my eyes to Your gifts, and then free me to give.*

*Now listen, you who say, "Today or tomorrow we will go to this or that city, spend a year there, carry on business and make money." Why, you do not even know what will happen tomorrow.*
*James 4:13, 14a*

We like to take life in leaps and bounds. We like to make sure that everything is safe. But we find out that life is indefinite, that it is filled with a delicious ambiguity.

Life is a daily thing. By that I mean that no matter how we like to break up life to ease the burden, it still keeps falling into a day-to-day pattern. We have invented weeks, months, and years, but we can't live them. They only work in your Day-Timers for scheduling. When it comes to actually living life, it's a daily sort of thing. We can only do it one day at a time, and it can never be "fixed." There will always be some heartache.

---

*Lord, I don't know what tomorrow will bring, but I do know that You will be there in my tomorrow.*

*Peace I leave with you; my peace I give you. I do not give to you as the world gives. Do not let your hearts be troubled and do not be afraid.*
*John 14:27*

I cannot tell you how things should be; I can only tell you how I feel and what I have experienced. Although sometimes overwhelmed by confusion, I remain hopeful. Although sometimes overcome by loneliness, I still believe. I not only don't have all the answers, I'm sometimes not even sure I'm asking the right questions. Life is more complicated than I ever imagined. God's presence has brought peace, not certainty.

*You promised Your peace, Lord, in the midst of uncertainty. Thank You.*

*I pray that you, being rooted and established in love, may have power, together with all the saints, to grasp how wide and long and high and deep is the love of Christ . . . that you may be filled to the measure of all the fullness of God.*
*Ephesians 3:17b, 18, 19b*

A broken heart simply contains more room for love. In my own personal dark night of the soul, it felt like the vacuum within me was getting bigger and bigger. Then I realized that this "hollowness" was simply creating more room and more appetite for God. My cup of emptiness became a Cup for His Presence and His Love.

We must remain "empty" in our loneliness (that is, not trying to fill it with every possible distraction), or He cannot fill us.

And this love that He gives is pure gift. Therefore we must struggle through the mine field of our doubts to open our hearts to gratitude.

*Fill the lonely, empty place of my soul with Your presence, God.*

*For John the Baptist came in the strictest austerity and you say he is crazy. Then the Son of Man came, enjoying life, and you say, "Look, a drunkard and a glutton, a bosom friend of the tax collector and the outsider!"*
*Luke 7:33, 34 (Phillips)*

Occasionally, our lives are too neat and tidy for God to be able to invade our situations. As James Dittes said, "Perhaps it is just to a divided nation, a ruptured community, a torn family, a split self, a chaotic sense of vocation, and an impossible church that Christ and His call comes most profoundly."

It is in the middle of our brokenness, in our overwhelming frustration over unsolvable problems, in our despair, in our anguish, in our doubts that Christ comes most fully.

*I'd rather have neat and tidy than chaos and brokenness, Lord. But most of all, I long for the reality of You.*

✸

*Then Peter got down out of the boat and walked*
*on the water and came toward Jesus. But when*
*he saw the wind, he was afraid and, beginning*
*to sink, cried out, "Lord, save me!"*
*Matthew 14:29b, 30*

Peter can teach us a lot about unsolvable problems. When Jesus walked on the Sea of Galilee, Peter demonstrated unusual audacity. Joining Jesus on the water, he was doing all right—until he lost his focus on Jesus and began to concentrate on "water walking." In his fearfulness, he sank.

Funny thing about Peter, rather than treading water, swimming back to the boat, or heading for the shore, he simply looked to Jesus and uttered one of the shortest prayers you can: "Lord, help me!"

Jesus didn't say, "Sorry, Peter, that was a pretty poor prayer." Instead, Jesus reached out and caught him.

Sometimes the best we can do is to place our focus on Jesus and cry out, "Lord, help me!"

✸ ——————————————————

*Jesus, I see Your hand reaching out to me,*
*and I too cry, "Lord, help me."*

***Elijah was afraid and ran for his life. When he came to Beersheba in Judah, he left his servant there, while he himself went a day's journey into the desert. He came to a broom tree, sat down under it and prayed that he might die.***
***I Kings 19:3, 4a***

Many of our biblical heroes experienced loneliness.

Elijah, frustrated after his great conquest over the gods of Baal, cried out, "I am the only one." Abraham must have felt incredibly alone when he was asked to sacrifice his only son, Isaac. Moses knew what it was to feel alone, and through that discovered a God that he wanted to know personally. The apostle Paul cried out, "Send me Barnabas!" to ease the pain of his loneliness.

I think that these experiences were written about in Scripture to remind us not to fear loneliness, but to have the courage to go through it. The way out is through!

*Father, I want to run from the loneliness, not walk through it. I look to You for courage.*

❈

*Hear my prayer, O Lord; let my cry for help
come to you. Do not hide your face from me
when I am in distress. Turn your ear to me; when
I call, answer me quickly. . . . I am like a desert
owl, like an owl among the ruins. I lie awake; I
have become like a bird alone on a roof.*
**Psalm 102:1, 2, 6, 7**

Loneliness *need not* be an enemy . . . it can
be a friend.

*Loneliness need not* be an interruption in our
lives . . . it can be a gift.

*Loneliness need not* be an obstacle . . . it can be
an invitation.

*Loneliness need not* be a problem . . . it can be
an opportunity.

*Loneliness need not* be a dead end . . . it can be
an adventure!

As Clark Moustakas says, "I say let there be
loneliness, for where there is loneliness, there is
also sensitivity, there is awareness and recogni-
tion of promise."

❈ ──────────────────────────────

*Turn my loneliness into opportunity for the
work of Your Spirit, Lord.*

✿

*Let them give thanks to the Lord for his unfailing love and his wonderful deeds for men, for he satisfies the thirsty and fills the hungry with good things. Psalm 107:8, 9*

Loneliness does not always come from emptiness. Sometimes it is because I am too full . . . full of myself. Full of activity. Full of distractions. Paradoxically, if I want to heal the loneliness in my life, I've got to get away to be alone with God.

If God speaks to us anywhere, He speaks to us in our daily lives. What is your loneliness trying to say to you? Pascal's oft-quoted statement that within each of us is a God-shaped vacuum seems worth saying one more time. Is it possible that your loneliness is trying to remind you that there are some holes that only God can fill? What are two or three details of your life that you can turn over to God today?

✿ —————————————————————

*Father, it's as though I've been hoarding my problems for myself, hugging them to me. Here are some details of my life I release to You now.*

❧

*Don't you know what the Scripture says in the
passage about Elijah—how he appealed to God
against Israel: "Lord, they have killed your
prophets and torn down your altars; I am the
only one left, and they are trying to kill me"?
And what was God's answer to him? "I have
reserved for myself seven thousand who have not
bowed the knee to Baal." Romans 11:2b–4*

Loneliness is a wrinkled and unappreciated
feeling . . . like a well-worn pair of faded jeans.
It's the kind of feeling you find in the corner of
the closet when you're not even looking for it.
A leftover ache, rumpled in the corner—which
somehow manages to penetrate your whole
being.

Loneliness is like a caterpillar in a cocoon. It
feels abandoned and isolated, but it can be God's
way of preparing to give us new wings of
freedom.

❧ _____

*Sometimes I do feel like a wrinkled garment forgotten
in the corner of a closet. But You know where I am,
and You have not discarded me.*

✥

*For I am convinced that neither death nor life,*
*neither angels nor demons, . . . nor anything else*
*in all creation, will be able to separate us from*
*the love of God that is in Christ Jesus our Lord.*
*Romans 8:38, 39*

There is an acronym in wilderness survival literature that says STOP. Stop, Think, Observe, Prepare when you realize you are lost. Perhaps when we get lost on the inside, we need to use the acronym for a slightly different slogan: Surrender, Trust, Obey, Pray. We surrender our lostness, our loneliness to God as we lean into it, and thereby transform it into solitude. We must not keep trying to avoid the loneliness by constant distraction—by wandering here and there. He is here. He is here. He is here! We can push through the loneliness to joy.

✥ ———————————————————————

*It's easy to forget, Lord, that You never leave me—*
*even the times when I feel lost and lonely inside.*

*As soon as Jesus was baptized, he went up out of the water. At that moment heaven was opened, and he saw the Spirit of God descending like a dove and lighting on him. And a voice from heaven said, "This is my Son, whom I love; with him I am well pleased." Then Jesus was led by the Spirit into the desert to be tempted by the devil. Matthew 3:16–4:1*

In the pain of our loneliness God says, "You are My child in whom I'm well pleased. Now I'm going to lead you through the desert so that you can taste Me, touch Me, see Me, hear Me in new ways."

Loneliness is not a time of abandonment . . . it just feels that way. It's actually a time of encounter at new levels with the only One who can fill that empty place in our hearts.

*Let me feel Your hand in mine,*
*guiding me through this desert place.*

✦

*In my distress I called to the Lord . . . my cry
came before him, into his ears. . . . He parted the
heavens and came down; dark clouds were under
his feet. He mounted the cherubim and flew; he
soared on the wings of the wind. He made darkness his covering, his canopy around him.*
*Psalm 18:6, 9–11a*

As I hiked down the mountain it was getting dark, and my senses came alive in extraordinary ways. I listened intently to every sound.
My eyes adjusted so I could see in the fading
light. I felt my muscles more intensely.

I realized that I liked the darkness. I didn't
need to avoid it. I could see the light where the
camp was, and I could feel my way back.

So, too, with the dark times of our soul. If
only we are not afraid to relax in the present
and become more aware, there is enough light
to walk in the darkness of our inner wilderness.

✦ ——————————————————————

*I peer through the dark night of my soul,
longing for a glimpse of Your light.*

*Now faith is being sure of what we hope for and certain of what we do not see. Hebrews 11:1*

The Bible is a wilderness book. It talks a lot about faith. And faith is always a leap into the uncharted. You can't tiptoe across a chasm, nor can you take it in two leaps. Faith is the ultimate gamble. It takes immense courage.

The wilderness is unknown. It is unpredictable. We go into our interior wilderness in order to learn, to discover, to grow. We never know what will happen. We're boldly asking God to surprise us, overwhelm us, stun us again with His presence and His love.

> *That's where faith begins . . . in the wilderness, when you are all alone and afraid, when things don't make any sense.*
> ELISABETH ELLIOT

*When I feel alone, when life doesn't make sense, surprise me with Your presence. Overwhelm me with Your love.*

❧

*Our God, who is full of kindness through Christ, will give you his eternal glory. He personally will come and pick you up, and set you firmly in place, and make you stronger than ever.*
*I Peter 5:10 (TLB)*

Having spent so much time in the wilderness, I can see that it is a marvelous metaphor for our inner journey . . . our spiritual pilgrimage . . . our "journey of the heart." In many ways, the interior wilderness is infinitely more difficult and complex.

In Scripture a wilderness experience always has a distinct purpose and it always leads to a promise. The same is true of the interior wilderness; it is likewise a time of radical dependence, of training for a purpose and, if we go through it, it will also lead to a promise. It has a gift hidden within.

❧ ────────────────────────────

*Lord, help me discover the gift hidden in*
*my wilderness experience.*

❄

*Blessed are those whose strength is in you, who have set their hearts on pilgrimage. Psalm 84:5*

Some people are never lonely, right? Like extroverts—they're never lonely. And how could married people know the pain of loneliness? Surely beautiful people aren't ever lonely. And successful people—they don't even have time to be lonely.

The media would have us believe that there are certain people who have somehow missed the anguish and confusion that loneliness brings to the rest of us.

In the midst of our loneliness, we often feel like we're the only ones. But the truth is that to be human is to know loneliness firsthand. Although each of us is as unique as our fingerprints, we have all known at times the ache of loneliness. It is part of the human condition.

❄ _____

*Abba, Father, You are my comfort, my strength, and my companion in the lonely times of life.*

❧

*I call on the Lord in my distress, and he
answers me. Psalm 120:1*

I have thought at times that there is no
pain quite so empty as loneliness. It is the pain
of simply being alive. We've all tasted it. There is
no life without relationships—and there can be
no relationships without loneliness. Loneliness
and love are inseparable twins.

Loneliness may be one of the most difficult
experiences that any of us will have to face. It's
that inner vacuum that nothing seems to be able
to fill. A void. An emptiness. An ache that nothing is able to fix. A pain that is elusive, evasive.

But as we journey from loneliness to love, we
can do it through the tunnel of solitude—where
we again discover that God loves us truly and
fully for who we are and not who we think we
should be.

❧ _____

*I praise You, Father God, when in my loneliness
You lead me to the solitude of Your presence.*

*Because God wanted to make the unchanging nature of his purpose very clear to the heirs of what was promised, he confirmed it with an oath. God did this so that, by two unchangeable things in which it is impossible for God to lie, we who have fled to take hold of the hope offered to us may be greatly encouraged. We have this hope as an anchor for the soul, firm and secure. Hebrews 6:17–19a*

Mine is only a muffled triumph,
Joy mingled with still-ever-constant pain
an unjustifiable gladness
of merely being alive.
The daily confrontations often leave me
Less than the best.
But still
Something ever new keeps emerging
Hope—now deeper, more enduring
Love—yes, but in unsentimental dailiness
Faith—not enough to move mountains
But just enough to keep me
in muffled triumph.

*You are my anchor, God, my hope
when I can only faintly celebrate.*

❧

*If you do this you will experience God's peace,
which is far more wonderful than the human
mind can understand. His peace will keep your
thoughts and your hearts quiet and at rest as you
trust in Christ Jesus. Philippians 4:7 (TLB)*

Joy is a process, a journey—often muffled,
sometimes detoured; a mystery in which we
participate, not a product we can grasp. It grows
and regenerates as we have the courage to let go
and trust the process. Growth and joy are inhib-
ited when we say "if only," enhanced when we
realize that failures and difficulties are not only a
critical part of the process, but are our very
opportunities to grow.

When we give up our excessive need for
security and "clean victories," for everything to
be right, then the peace that passes all understanding has room to invade our lives again.

❧ _____

*Once again, O God, I am relying on Your peace in
the midst of the failures and difficulties.*

❀

*One thing I do know. I was blind but now I see!*
*John 9:25b*

What we have traditionally perceived as limitations are sometimes the lens which can bring our life into deeper and finer focus.

Caught once in a terrible fog, I realized that I couldn't see anything in the distance. So I took advantage of the situation, slowed down, and relished the beauty that was close at hand.

In a world that inundates us with choices, one can become disoriented and almost over-whelmed by too many options. Life can become thinned out by trying to do too many things. One of the advantages of disadvantages is the privilege of being forced to see that which is closer, that which is simple, that which has been given to you. Life must have limitations in order to have depth.

❀ _____

*Lord, thank You for the way my problems can give my life a deeper focus.*

✹

*I have told you these things, so that in me you may have peace. In this world you will have trouble. But take heart! I have overcome the world. John 16:33*

There is no question that life is difficult. In fact, it has been said that God promises four things: peace, power, purpose, and TROUBLE. For example, in the verse above Jesus reminds us quite boldly that in the world there will be trouble. But we are not merely to endure it. We are to "be of good cheer," for He has overcome the world.

Many of us have only gotten half the message. We recognize the difficulty of life and drearily drag ourselves through each day, mumbling about our burdens. (I've heard it said that "some Christians have just enough Christianity to make them miserable.") It can be different—but the choice is ours.

✹ _____

*You promised both peace and trouble, Jesus. But You also promised that I could have them at the same time. Thank You!*

*It is for freedom that Christ has set us free.*
*Stand firm, then, and do not let yourselves*
*be burdened again by a yoke of slavery.*
**Galatians 5:1**

I find that I can feel guilty about most anything these days—being overweight, being overtired, being distracted by pain, not being able to perform as I used to. It's an ongoing battle. Perhaps one of the best things I've ever read about guilt was this simple statement: "No one benefits from your guilt." This simple fact, more than any other, has forced me to let go of some of the guilt that I seem to want to carry around.

My guilt, your guilt, benefits no one. Although it's a natural phenomenon, and a common byproduct of pain, we need to do anything we can to let go of it. We are who we are. The past is just that—proof. We can choose freedom.

*How it lifts my spirits to realize that You have set me free from guilt. I choose that freedom with gratitude.*

*Turn to me and be gracious to me, for I am
lonely and afflicted. The troubles of my heart
have multiplied; free me from my anguish.
Psalm 25:16, 17*

Next to the genuine fatigue of pain, possibly the most energy-depriving thing I know is self-pity. I know from firsthand experience that it is one of the greatest wastes of my time and emotions, yet I confess my vulnerability to it.

My greatest need at these times is for people who will listen to me compassionately, but then firmly and gently encourage me out of such dreadful behavior. It is important that people don't join me in my self-pity party, but love me into remembering what I can do and must do.

The sooner I let go of self-pity and get on with living, the better off I am.

*Thank You, God, for the people You have
sent along the way who will not allow me
to wallow in self-pity.*

❊

*I waited patiently for the Lord; he turned to me
and heard my cry. He lifted me out of the slimy
pit, out of the mud and mire; he set my feet on a
rock and gave me a firm place to stand.*
*Psalm 40:1, 2*

You don't truly discover your roots until
you are at the bottom of the pit. From this perspective you are no longer distracted by usual
superficialities which disguise themselves in
masks of importance. The word *root* means "to
dig down in some mass in order to find something valuable. In higher orders of living things
a means of support, a reservoir of life energy.
The cause, the source, the essence, the essential
points or parts . . ." And, finally, it means "to be
or become firmly established, to plant or fix
deeply," as in the earth. At the bottom of the pit
God can teach us to rediscover the substance of
our strength and song.

❊ ───────────────────────

*At the bottom of the pit, Lord, I look up and see
Your hand stretched down to me.*

❧

*Never will I leave you; never will I forsake you.*
*Hebrews 13:5b*

Some problems will remain unresolved. Some hopes will never be fulfilled. Some dreams will never be accomplished. Some problems are just not meant to be solved in this life.

Joy is not the same as happiness. Jesus did not promise that a Christian's life would be free of troubles and problems. He did not promise us happiness, health, or success. Nor did He promise that our relationships would last forever.

Jesus promised us joy and eternal life, and He promised us that He would always be with us.

*Jesus, what more could I need than Your "always" presence? I cling to that promise.*

# In Quietness
## and
## Confidence

🔱

*It is senseless for you to work so hard from early morning until late at night, fearing you will starve to death; for God wants his loved ones to get their proper rest. Psalm 127:2 (TLB)*

We live in a world of unprecedented change, eruption, and above all else, hurry. It's a world that demands first of all a deep, quality relationship with Jesus Christ. The Enemy has done an effective job of convincing us that unless a person is worn to a frazzle, running here and there, he or she cannot possibly be a dedicated, sacrificing, spiritual Christian.

But there is hope. The world, ultimately, is God's responsibility. We are called to be faithful, not frantic. If we are to meet the challenges of today, there must be integrity between our words and our lives, and more reliance on the source of our purpose.

🔱 ────────────────────────

*Lord, it feels as though my life is a constant movement—hurrying from one thing to the next. Stop me, Lord. Help me reevaluate.*

*You are my lamp, O Lord; the Lord turns my
darkness into light. II Samuel 22:29*

To show the splendor of the newborn
Savior in the christmas pageant, an electric light
bulb was hidden in the manger. All the stage
lights were to be turned off so only the bright-
ness of the manger could be seen, but the boy
who controlled the lights got confused, and
suddenly all the lights went out. It was a fairly
tense moment broken by a little shepherd's loud
whisper, "Hey, you just switched off Jesus!"

I switch off Jesus much more than I am willing to admit. If you and I were to switch Jesus
back on in our lives, what would He be saying
to us? Prayer is listening to Him, not just telling
Him what we need.

As you listen to God, be willing to take the
steps that He has prepared for you. Allow God
to direct you and to be fully Himself in your
life.

*Let me be conscious of the times I turn off Your light
in my life. I need the illumination of Your Spirit.*

❀

*Let everything that has breath praise the Lord.*
*Praise the Lord. Psalm 150:6*

The rolling peaks of the Appalachians are so different from the rugged Sierra Nevadas. I walk along a pathway which cuts a swath through high grass and hay bales. On the ridge are silhouetted trees, leafless, waiting for spring.

I see a deer pause in the pathway. I wait and watch her delicate, hesitant movements. When she finally crosses the path, I notice another head pop out near the pathway—her fawn.

I am absolutely alone out here. There isn't another human being for miles, yet I do not feel lonely. Out here there is a greater sense of God's presence. It's almost tangible. Perhaps it is because there is less to distract me.

I think my own psalm: Let all things praise Him. Let the hills praise Him. Let the birds praise Him and the grass praise Him and the deer praise Him. Praise the Lord!

❀ _____

*Praise You, Lord! My whole being shouts*
*in glad praise to You!*

*You are my God, and I will give you thanks; you are my God, and I will exalt you. Psalm 118:28*

George Herbert once said, "Thou who has given me so much, give me one thing more—a grateful heart." Nothing makes us feel separate from God more than what has sometimes been called the ugliest of sins, ingratitude. But on the opposite side, nothing creates more intimacy with God than genuine gratitude. Are you spending time alone with Him reading Scripture, praying, and sometimes just listening to what He wants to say to you? What are five words that describe your spiritual life right now? If you had a shovel, in what areas of your life would you start digging in order to create a deeper relationship with God? It takes hard work. Nothing comes easy.

*Oh God, You know the places in my life that need digging out to create a deeper relationship with You. Give me courage to pick up the shovel and begin.*

❧

*Be joyful always; pray continually.*
*I Thessalonians 5:16, 17*

In your experience, how does God speak most clearly to you? Maybe it's while you're reading Scripture. Maybe it's in those quiet moments you have in your car on the way to work. God can speak to us anytime, anyplace. We don't have to be stopped altogether, but we do have to have a quiet, attentive, and eager heart.

Prayer is one of the most mysterious and powerful facets of our Christian walk. Without it our Christian life unravels. Prayer is the key, the core, the essence, the glue. A Christian without prayer is like a body without a heart or a car without an engine. It might look great, but it has no power and is certainly not going anywhere.

❧ ——————————————

*Why is it, God, that sometimes I ignore You? I don't talk to You. I don't listen for Your voice. Forgive me for letting the details of my life crowd You out.*

*After the earthquake came a fire, but the Lord
was not in the fire. And after the fire came a
gentle whisper. When Elijah heard it, he pulled
his cloak over his face and went out and stood at
the mouth of the cave. I Kings 19:12, 13a*

Elijah's challenge to the prophets of Baal
on Mt. Carmel became the Bible's biggest bar-
becue. He boldly challenged all four hundred
and fifty prophets to see whose God was real.

You know the outcome. It was the most
stunning success of Elijah's career.

But circumstances changed. Jezebel came after
Elijah with a vengeance. Hiding from her, he
finally said, "I've had enough, Lord. Take my
life." He felt alone and afraid.

Then God spoke, "Go out and stand on the
mountain in the presence of the Lord, for the
Lord is about to pass by." But God was not in
the powerful wind, earthquake, or fire that
followed. "After the fire came a gentle whisper."

That was how God came to Elijah.

*Help me to be quiet enough to hear
Your gentle whisper, God.*

❀

*After [Jesus] had dismissed them, he went up a*
*mountainside by himself to pray. When evening*
*came, he was there alone. Matthew 14:23*

Making life happen means: making time
to think, for it is the source of power; making
time to play, because it is the source of freedom,
relaxation, and the secret of youth. It is making
time to read, for that is the foundation of
knowledge, making time to worship, for that is
the pathway of blessing, and washes the dust of
earth from our eyes. It is making time to help
and enjoy friends, for there is no other happiness that can match this. It is making time to
love, for if you don't, love will fade away. It is
making time to laugh and pray, for those are the
two things that lighten life's loads.

And making life happen means making time
to be alone with God, which is not only the
greatest privilege of life, but the source of
everything else we do.

❀ ────────────────────────────

*You needed time alone with the Father, Jesus. How*
*much more, how very much more, do I!*

❧

*But Martha was distracted by all the preparations that had to be made. She came to him and asked, "Lord, don't you care that my sister has left me to do the work by myself? Tell her to help me!" "Martha, Martha," the Lord answered, "you are worried and upset about many things. . . ."* Luke 10:40, 41

One morning I was on my way to coach a college football team. As usual, I'd tried to cram too much into the early morning hours. The car that made me pull over had a winking light and a somber man in blue who gave me a ticket. The charge: I had broken the law. I was hurrying too fast.

On my way to the game the Lord talked to me about my predicament. *You broke the law.* I agreed. *No, you still don't understand. You broke The Law.*

The worst part was not breaking an external, man-made law—although that is serious enough—but breaking a far greater, eternal rhythm. I had submitted to the sin of hurry.

❧ _____

*In these crammed-full days, please help me to slow down to listen for You.*

❧

*. . . that out of his glorious, unlimited resources
he will give you the mighty inner strengthening
of his Holy Spirit. Ephesians 3:16 (TLB)*

Most of us do not know how to handle
leisure, nor do we understand its true meaning
and purpose.

To many, the word leisure has an unsubstan-
tial sound. It confuses us, and therefore we mis-
trust it. Picture postcards cast glamour over
places to go and things to do, but the nature
and essence of true leisure eludes us. Often this
confusion makes us turn leisure into work.
Motivated by a false sense of guilt, we transform
what should be a joyous weekend release into a
Monday-morning exhaustion. We turn pleasur-
able games into hard-fought contests.

We have yet to learn that true leisure is not
idleness, and that it can be a touchstone with
ourselves and the inner resources God has given
each of us.

❧ _____

*Show me how to use leisure times to get in touch
with the inner resources You've given me, Father.*

❈

*Draw near to God and He will draw
near to you. James 4:8a (NASB)*

The Western mind and culture leave little
time for leisure, prayer, play, and contemplation.
Hurry needs answers; answers need categories; categories need labeling and dissecting.

Hurry gives us an "excuse" for our lack of spiritual growth. Only by breaking the chains of busyness can we escape the prison of status quo, and experience a life that draws ever nearer to God.

No matter how "good" our purpose is, a driven person is still enslaved and cannot act freely, thoughtfully, lovingly. The good becomes the enemy of the best. Henry David Thoreau offered first prize to the person who could live one day deliberately. But this is not an easily accomplished task.

Quiet minds, which are established in stillness, refuse to be perplexed or intimidated. They are like a clock in a thunderstorm, which moves at its own pace.

❈ _____

*God, break the chains of busyness and set me on a
quest for the quiet where You are waiting.*

❀

*Yet you are near, O Lord, and all your
commands are true. Psalm 119:151*

Loneliness is not the same as being alone.
Loneliness is feeling alone no matter how many
people are around you. It is a feeling of being
disconnected, unplugged, left out, isolated.
Unfortunately, you can't buy anything over the
counter to cure it.

Loneliness occurs deep down within us, and
the only hope for a solution must also come
from that deep-down suchness of a place and a
Person. Through conversation and presence we
can turn loneliness into something powerful.
Prayer is our means of conversation with God,
and solitude is our opportunity for experiencing
His inner presence. And how do we experience
His presence? We must stop to recognize how
near He is.

❀ _____

*What comfort, God, to know that You are nearer
than the loneliness I feel deep within me.*

✺

*My sheep listen to my voice; I know them,
and they follow me. John 10:27*

An Indian walking along with his friend in
New York City suddenly said, "I hear a cricket."

"You're crazy," his friend replied.

"No, I hear a cricket. I'm sure of it."

"It's noon. There are people bustling around,
cars honking, taxis squealing!"

"I'm sure I hear a cricket." He listened, walked
to the corner, crossed the street, and began digging
beneath the shrubs in a large planter until he
found the cricket.

The Indian said to his amazed friend, "My ears
are no different from yours. It simply depends on
what you are listening to. Here, let me show you."

He reached into his pocket, pulled out a hand-
ful of change, and dropped it on the concrete.
Every head nearby turned.

"See what I mean?" the Indian said as he began
picking up his coins. "It all depends on what you
are listening for."

✺ ─────────────────────────────

*Jesus, quiet the clamor within.
I want to listen for Your voice.*

*I will be with you constantly until I have
finished giving you all I am promising.*
**Genesis 28:15b (TLB)**

St. Augustine said, "O Lord, my heart is
restless until it finds its rest in Thee." God, too,
must ache with our restlessness. I wonder if He,
too, doesn't long to find His rest in us. And
there are so few people these days in whom He
can find rest.

In the midst of my bewilderment, I am struggling to be one of those people. If we are not
afraid of our loneliness, it can lead us to dimensions of our lives that we never knew existed
before. If we will allow our loneliness to teach
us, we will discover again that we are truly not
alone—we can know an Inner Presence and
hope that transcends anything that a mere mortal can give.

*Your inner presence, oh Holy One, calls me
to rest in You. Teach me in that quiet
center where You wait.*

※

*As the deer pants for streams of water, so my soul*
*pants for you, O God. Psalm 42:1*

Sometimes there's nothing quite as desperate as feeling all alone. Trapped in your own isolation, it feels like you are in a house with all the windows blackened out so that there is no sunlight coming through. There is an inner darkness that can't seem to be pushed out. There's a great truth that "when you can't push the darkness out, you can let the light in." We may be lonely, but we are not alone. Loneliness can be a unique gift from God—a vehicle through which we get to know Him better.

※ _____

*Now I can thank You for loneliness,*
*for through it I hear You calling to me.*

❀

*Be still before the Lord and wait*
*patiently for him. Psalm 37:7a*

Loneliness is an ache that sometimes feels like it cannot be relieved. It tends to be a time of withdrawal, a time when we become preoccupied with our own emptiness. However, loneliness can also be an unexpected invitation to discover God's love and mercy at a previously unexplored level.

Loneliness can be a gift from God. A gift that opens up our heart to yearn for His peace. It can lead us to a deeper experience of His presence.

❀ —————————————————————

*Being still before You does not come naturally, Lord.*
*Please, teach me how to be quiet within.*

*Yet the news about him spread all the more, so that crowds of people came to hear him and to be healed of their sicknesses. But Jesus often withdrew to lonely places and prayed. Luke 5:15, 16*

In our search for solitude we can overlook some simple opportunities—like the automobile. Sometimes when I'm driving alone I empty the seat beside me and make a place for Jesus. Then we carry on a conversation in the moving solitude. I'm sure some drivers going past must think I'm crazy, talking to myself, but who cares? (I have a dear friend who is constantly saying to me, "Let them think you're loony!") These moments turn out to be some of the most special times of my day.

What opportunities for solitude have you been missing?

*I need to find times and places to be completely alone with You, God. Inspire my imagination to sort out where and when.*

❧

*Be still, and know that I am God; I will*
*be exalted among the nations, I will be*
*exalted in the earth. Psalm 46:10*

For eighteen years I directed the wilderness
ministry of Summit Expedition. It is interesting
to note that although our wilderness courses
were incredibly adventurous, perhaps the greatest change in individual lives came during what
we called "solo"—a time when the participant
is alone with God. Many people said, "No wonder lives are changed so dramatically given all
the adventurous things you do." I reminded
them that lives are changed most when we sit
still in the presence of God—that is the Great
Adventure.

❧

*God, my Father, I wait here in the stillness*
*for Your life-changing voice.*

*The fruit of righteousness will be peace;
the effect of righteousness will be quietness
and confidence forever. Isaiah 32:17*

As long as we are busy, busy, busy, we never have to face what is really important in life. We never have to find out who God really is. We simply follow the God we have underlined in the Bible—not the God who is, but the God we want Him to be. All we have to do is carefully ignore anything in Scripture that doesn't meet our specifications of God—and never spend time alone with Him. We can be busy at work, busy at home, and busy at church. All work equally well at helping us ignore God as He really is.

Solitude is a flower born of simplicity. It needs to be tended slowly and patiently. A quiet heart never comes easy, never in a hurry.

*Oh God, I am busy doing good and important
things that have often crowded You out. I need
help to even want to tend to solitude.*

❄

*And if you leave God's paths and go astray, you will hear a Voice behind you say, "No, this is the way; walk here." Isaiah 30:21 (TLB)*

Our life of action must come from our commitment to stillness. In fact the root of the world "obedience" is *obadare*, which means "to listen."

Mother Teresa won a Nobel Peace Prize for her work in Calcutta. It is important to note that Mother Teresa is first of all a contemplative. She is first of all committed to a life of prayer. Her action in the world comes from her reckless receivership from God, from her direct relationship with God.

Our prayer life is where we make the deep connection to the living Christ. As we listen, He directs.

❄ ⎯⎯⎯⎯⎯⎯⎯⎯⎯⎯⎯⎯⎯⎯⎯⎯⎯⎯⎯

*Living Christ, grow in me a desire to make quiet, listening prayer a priority.*

*Hear my cry, O God; listen to my prayer. From the ends of the earth I call to you, I call as my heart grows faint; lead me to the rock that is higher than I. For you have been my refuge, a strong tower against the foe. I long to dwell in your tent forever and take refuge in the shelter of your wings. Psalm 61:1-4*

Loneliness is the gift that leads us to solitude—and without solitude, the Christian life is impossible. Loneliness parches our lips for the living God, makes us hungry for His presence.

Loneliness reminds us that we were made by God—for God—that our loneliness can be transformed into solitude, which can and will teach us about genuine, inextinguishable love.

Solitude makes us see things that we couldn't see before. Solitude invites the inner presence of God. It's about as obvious and reasonable as daylight. And as magnificent.

*Dear Father, I am discovering that there is nothing better than being in solitude with You.*

∿

*The apostles now rejoined Jesus and reported to
him all that they had done and taught. He said
to them, "Come with me, by yourselves, to some
lonely place where you can rest quietly."*
*Mark 6:30,31 (NEB)*

I don't understand how the Master could
take time to go into the desert to fast and pray
when countless individuals needed Him . . . but
He did. I don't understand how He could tell us
not to worry about life when times are so difficult. I don't understand how He could say that
sometimes it is better just to sit at His feet than
to be up doing things for Him. Or how He
could promise rest in the midst of a world filled
with turmoil and distorted with pain. I don't
understand how Jesus could play and celebrate
and enjoy life, when the world was in the condition it was in. I don't understand . . . but He
did.

∿ _____

*In the midst of a world filled with turmoil and pain,
I sit at Your feet, Jesus.*

*I am still confident of this: I will see the
goodness of the Lord in the land of the living.
Wait for the Lord; be strong and take heart
and wait for the Lord. Psalm 27:13, 14*

We have allowed ourselves to be intoxicated by bigness. We sometimes anticipate that God can only speak to us through a spectacular event. We fail to realize that most of God's miracles are small, and that He often chooses to speak to us in a still, small voice.

What is God trying to say to you these days? Perhaps He is saying, "Slow down." Perhaps He is reminding you that "to obey is better than sacrifice." Perhaps He is gently trying to encourage you with His persistent love. Perhaps He is hoping that you will recall the extent of His forgiveness. Perhaps He is whispering to you in your loneliness—and it is an invitation to a deeper experience with Him.

*Have I ever been quiet enough inside to really hear
You, God? I wait here in the stillness for Your voice.*

❋

*I will listen to what God the Lord will say; he*
*promises peace to his people, his saints.*
*Psalm 85:8a*

I had a high-school teacher who, when he
wanted to be heard, would lower his voice. As
the din in the room would get louder and louder, he would lower his voice almost to a whisper. When he did that, the entire class began to
focus intently upon him, quieting down to a
hush so they could hear him in his whispering
voice.

God wants to speak to us. Sometimes He
shouts to us through difficult circumstances;
more often than we realize, He is whispering to
us in our daily lives.

❋ ────────────────────────────

*Open my inner ears to hear You in the*
*circumstances of this day.*

❧

*He who dwells in the shelter of the Most High*
*will rest in the shadow of the Almighty.*
*Psalm 91:1*

God has spoken very boldly about His desire to be a presence in our lives. If I want to heal the ache and loneliness in my own life, one of the things I need to do is get away alone with God. The paradoxical "answer" to loneliness is aloneness . . . with God. In the silence God speaks most powerfully. Too often His words get muffled, lost, or covered by the crowd of many noises both inside and outside of us. We must have a quiet heart in order to hear God's distinctive message.

❧ ——————————————————————

*Lord, even when I shut out the outside noises,*
*I need Your help to quiet my noisy soul.*

❧

*I am the Lord your God, who brought you up
out of Egypt. Open wide your mouth and
I will fill it. Psalm 81:10*

Sometimes we need to pull away from
other people to explore our feelings and discover again that we are fearfully and wonderfully
made, complex for a purpose.

Loneliness is like holding a cup upside down
under a faucet that is open full blast. The cup
cannot be filled because we are not ready to
receive. Solitude is when we turn the cup over
to receive, to be filled. No one, not even God
Himself, can turn that cup over for us. We alone
must make the choice to receive God's grace
and inner presence.

❧ ───────────────────────────

*Here I am, Lord, waiting in the solitude
for the fullness of Your presence.*

＊

*O God, you are my God, earnestly I seek you;*
*my soul thirsts for you, my body longs for you, in*
*a dry and weary land where there is no water.*
*Psalm 63:1*

A boy watched a holy man praying on the banks of a river. When he finished praying the boy went over and asked him, "Will you teach me to pray?"

The holy man studied the boy's face. Then he gripped the boy's head in his hands and plunged it into the water. The boy struggled frantically, until finally the holy man released his hold.

When the boy was able to catch his breath, he gasped, "What did you do that for?"

"When you long to pray as much as you longed to breathe when your head was underwater," said the holy man, "only then will I be able to teach you to pray."

When we want God more than anything—more than success, more than peace, more than health—then we truly know how to pray; then we discover Him in fullness.

＊

*My loving Father God, instill in me a longing for*
*You that transcends all else in my life.*

*Blessed are those who have learned to acclaim you, who walk in the light of your presence, O Lord. Psalm 89:15*

Many who have walked with the Lord over a period of years encourage us to spend time in prayer and solitude, but most of us feel like we can't find the time or the place.

In our search for solitude, we have inadvertently overlooked some of the simple opportunities that surround us all. There's no such thing as "perfect" solitude. We are surrounded by moments of solitude, if we would only see them. Brother Lawrence wrote about practicing the presence of God while doing the most mundane human chores.

Since the love of God was the end of all his actions, he simply established the habit of conversing with God continually, wherever he was and whatever he was doing. Through that he developed "the habitual sense of God's presence."

*Teach me how to be in Your presence, consciously, as I experience this day.*

❋

*But as for me, I will always have hope; I will praise you more and more. My mouth will tell of your righteousness, of your salvation all day long, though I know not its measure. Psalm 71:14, 15*

God uses
What you have
to fill a need which
you never could have filled.
God uses
where you are
to take you where
you never could have gone.
God uses what you can do
to accomplish what
you never could have done.
God uses
who you are
to let you become who
you never could have been.

—Philip Clarke Brewer

❋ _____

*I'm not sure where Your life within is taking me, God. But I have hope, because You make possible what could not otherwise be.*

179

*Abide in me, and I in you.*
*John 15:4a (KJV)*

In *The Province Beyond the River*, W. Paul Jones writes about his courageous journey . . . three months of solitude in a remote Trappist monastery in the mountains of Colorado. It is a powerful account of self-discovery and transcendence. Having spent his whole life reading, teaching, thinking, and writing "about" God, Jones in his own words admits that he had never really experienced God. Though he was a professing Christian, he admitted to being a "functional atheist."

We need to ask ourselves, "Do I really know what it means to practice the presence of God? Have I really experienced God in the way He wants me to?"

---

*I want to be honest about my true experience of You,*
*God. I want to grow in my awareness of You,*
*in my experience of You.*

☙

*For everything that was written in the past was written to teach us, so that through endurance and the encouragement of the Scriptures we might have hope. Romans 15:4*

The camel is one of God's funniest-looking creatures with its long, spindly legs, too-long feet, long neck holding a too-big head, and drooping nose.

But the thing that stands out most is the hump—the big, dumb, ugly hump—which is essential in the desert where more beautiful and streamlined beasts die quickly of thirst.

When we, like camels, develop our inner resources sufficiently, we can cross every wasteland and survive arid times without relying on the external. Those times of silence, those years of prayer on camel knees, that inner simplicity that we may consider inelegant—these will eventually be our oases, our secret wells of joy.

*Lord, do Your work in my Spirit. Make me willing to experience what I must to develop spiritual endurance.*

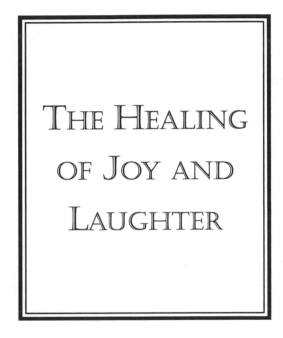

# THE HEALING
## OF JOY AND
## LAUGHTER

*Our mouths were filled with laughter, our tongues with songs of joy. Then it was said among the nations, "The Lord has done great things for them." Psalm 126:2*

Dr. Seuss, the famous author of children's books, said, "Humor has a tremendous place in a sordid world. It's more than just a laughing matter. If you can see things out of whack, then you can certainly see how things can be in whack."

Having fun releases us from the bondage of our circumstances and gives us the capacity to laugh at our problems—and at ourselves. Having fun doesn't automatically make the pressures go away, but it helps us view them with less tension.

As Christians, we are called to reproduce the abundant (and fun) life that Jesus expresses in and through us.

*For laughter, for joy, for fun, for life:*
*Lord, I thank You!*

❈

*Give, and it will be given to you. A good mea-sure, pressed down, shaken together and running over, will be poured into your lap. For with the measure you use, it will be measured to you.*
*Luke 6:38*

Sometimes we wait for the world to reach out to us. We falsely believe that our loneliness is caused by circumstances beyond our control. We somehow believe that the remedy is out of our hands, that it is the responsibility of other people or God. So we keep waiting for others to make friendly overtures to us.

Waiting for the world to come to you is a lonely place. And it takes a lot of courage some-times to reach out to others. But if you can't find joy, then the best thing to do is give it away to someone else who is more in need than you are. The joy will then double back to you in ways that you never expected.

❈ _____

*So many times, Father, I have given and then received double in return. I love Your arithmetic!*

*Delight yourself in the Lord and he will give you the desires of your heart. Psalm 37:4*

Making life fun makes problem solving fun and allows us to get excited about the challenges that face us. One way that God helps us not to be overwhelmed is by giving us a sense of humor.

Is there any way you can take any one of your problems, turn it around, and make it a little fun? Is it possible through the gift of God's grace to lighten up and even to celebrate some of the problems He has given you? Is it possible, if nothing else, to laugh at yourself?

Learn to invite joy and fun into your life and even into your problem-solving struggles. The Scriptures remind us to delight ourselves in the Lord.

*I love You, Lord. You are my delight.*

❧

*Yet in the towns of Judah and the streets of Jerusalem that are deserted, inhabited by neither men nor animals, there will be heard once more the sounds of joy and gladness.*
*Jeremiah 33:10b, 11a*

Fun is not necessarily the same as joy, but fun can intensify joy. In her book, *Choosing the Amusing*, Marilyn Meberg says, "God has given to each of us an incomparable medicine bag. In it is the divinely created ability to laugh at ourselves. . . . To utilize the contents of that bag is to experience healing for our minds, our souls, and our bodies."

When people ask me why I sometimes do crazy, funny things, I like to reply, "I can't help it: I'm a Christian." I hope that confuses people into realizing that Christians have more to celebrate than anybody in the world. Life can be fun, but we must make it so. Remember, as Steve Allen said, "Don't try to suppress laughter; if you do, it will go down and spread out around your hips."

❧ ───────────────────────────

*I praise You for funny bones and unsuppressed giggles.*

◆

*Pleasant words are a honeycomb, sweet to the soul and healing to the bones. Proverbs16:24*

Charlie Brown, the lovable cartoon character in "Peanuts," said, "I've developed a new philosophy. I only dread life one day at a time." Some people do that with problems; they only dread them one at a time. Others, however, really do dread life day by day.

Yet God has given Christians a different prescription for life. Having forgiven and accepted us by His love, God wants us to have fun and enjoy life. He wants us to have a joyful spirit when we approach our problems.

God has prescribed that we live joyfully. So take God's prescription for your life just as you would a doctor's. Liven up some of those dried bones and broken spirits; realize that God can and wants to generate a genuine joy within us.

◆ ────────────────────

*Bring healing to my spirit, oh God. Liven my dry bones and generate new joy in my soul.*

***

*I have come so that they may have life,*
*and have it to the full. John 10:10b*

I never cease to be amazed at so many unhappy people in a world that has so much to offer. What surprises me even more is the sight of so many Christians who have succumbed to busyness, unhappiness, tightness, and boredom. Many suffer from a nagging sense of guilt that no matter how much they do, it is never quite enough.

Is it possible that your days are hurrying by so fast that you don't fully taste them anymore? When was the last time you flew a kite, went for a bike ride, or made something with your hands? When was the last time you caught yourself enjoying life so deeply that you couldn't quite get the smile off your face? Chances are, it's been too long.

Christ is waiting for you to slow down long enough to relearn the meaning of words like wonder, joy, rest, and freedom.

***

*You who are calling me to wonder and joy, help me*
*to slow down enough to experience these gifts.*

❁

*He that is of a merry heart hath a*
*continual feast. Proverbs 15:15b (KJV)*

God has given us humor to lighten the load of life's burdens.

Humor can help an individual handle discouragement, difficulty, or defeat. A football coach who suffered defeat in a major game was asked when he felt the turning point occurred. He replied, "Right after the national anthem." That little bit of humor took the edge off the defeat.

Humor can ease strain, oil relationships, reduce tensions, relieve pressures, and generally enhance the quality of life. We all want to work with and for someone who appreciates humor and spend our lifetime with someone who has it. Students crave it from teachers, children thrive on it. Humor liberates. It can give us the freedom to be ourselves and to take risks. It allows us to be willing to be different and to be able to make a difference.

❁ ───────────────────────────

*How I thank You for the gift of humor, Lord.*

❀

*The Lord lives! Praise be to my Rock! Exalted
be God my Savior! Psalm 18:46*

Driving to West Virginia, a friend and I
came up behind a van. Some kids in the van put
a sign in the back window, "MAKE A FACE."
We made the best faces that we possibly could.
Then they came back with a sign with big, red
letters saying, "THANK YOU."

We decided to join in the fun. In big, bold
letters, we wrote, "MAKE A PIG FACE." The
kids laughed so hard that they steamed up the
windows. Then they did one of the best impressions of a pig face that I've ever seen.

I am convinced that God loves to laugh. And
He wants us to learn how to play as well as
pray.

Today don't forget to say thank you to God
for His love, His laughter, and His presence.

❀ ——————————————————————

*Thank You, God, for the laughter and
fun that You bring into my life.*

❧

*Great is his faithfulness; his loving kindness*
*begins afresh each day. Lamentations 3:23 (TLB)*

Unknowingly, some of us think we serve a
God who is stingy, who loves us only in proportion to how much we work for Him, who is
embarrassed by laughter and surprised by spontaneity. We have forgotten that each day is a
gift—we did nothing to deserve it. We've forgotten that each breath is a gift, and all the
work in the world won't give us more. We've
forgotten that the mark of a believer is not only
love but joy, wonder, appreciation, surprise, creativity, peace, tenacity, hope, simplicity, and even
play.

May God open us to the little things in life
so that our hearts don't grow old. May He teach
us to be supple and thirsty for the everyday
wonders of being alive—so that our minds
won't grow weary. May He help us not to have
to be so useful that we become useless.

---

*Oh, God, deliver me from a life of weariness*
*and uselessness where I ignore the everyday*
*wonders of being alive.*

*Do not deceive yourselves. If any one of you thinks he is wise by the standards of this age, he should become a "fool" so that he may become wise. For the wisdom of this world is foolishness in God's sight. I Corinthians 3:18, 19a*

The problems with taking ourselves too seriously are countless. Afraid to fail, we no longer risk. Afraid that someone will see behind our image, we no longer share. Afraid that we will appear to need help, we can no longer be vulnerable. Afraid to appear not religious enough to some, we no longer can confess. The tragic result of taking ourselves too seriously is that in our fear of becoming childlike, in our fear of becoming a fool for Christ, in our fear of being seen as we are, we discover all too late that it's impossible to be fully human and fully alive.

*I want to live! Please show me what it means to be fully human and fully alive because I am Yours, Lord.*

❧❧

*Some of his disciples said to one another,*
*"What does he mean by saying, 'In a little while*
*you will see me no more, and then after a little*
*while you will see me'. . . ?" John 16:17a*

I think two of the reasons most people
miss joy are (1) they have preconceived images
of what joy is supposed to be, and (2) they try
to cling to experiences that fit those images.

In the past years I've been forced to let go of
my preconceived images about God, about life,
about others, and about myself. I've discovered
that I am less—and more—than what I had
imagined: both more whole and more frag-
mented, stronger and more fragile, more selfish
and more capable of genuine love.

At least for me, it is less the victorious
Christian life than the notorious Christian life,
because it is constantly new, changing, different,
and far more powerful than anything I'd
dreamed it to be.

❧❧ ―――――――――――――――――――――――――

*God, You continue to surprise me whenever*
*I think I've figured out exactly what the*
*Christian life is all about.*

❀

*As the Father has loved me, so have I loved you. Now remain in my love. If you obey my commands, you will remain in my love, just as I have obeyed my Father's commands and remain in his love. I have told you this so that my joy may be in you and that your joy may be complete. John 15:9–11*

Ours is an age that wants to neatly wrap everything in plastic. We want answers, no process. We're trained to come to conclusions which, when captured, we can control. The only problem is that it doesn't work in every area of our lives.

To me, one of the most exciting things about the Christian faith is that we'll never fully understand it. One of the most attractive things about Jesus is that we can't fully comprehend Him. And one of the most important things I know about the joy He wants to give us is that it's different from what we think it is.

❀ ———————————————————————

*Jesus, Your desire that we would experience joy is one more confirmation of Your dazzling love.*
*Thank You!*

***He will yet fill your mouth with laughter and your lips with shouts of joy. Job 8:21***

One day I asked a friend what she thought the five most important ingredients were to being a quality human being. After a long and thoughtful pause, she said, "Humor, love, responsibility, courage, and humor." I tried to point out that she had already said humor, but she informed me that she meant exactly what she had said.

Humor has the unshakable ability to break life up into little pieces and make it livable. Laughter adds richness, texture, and color to otherwise ordinary days. It is a gift, a choice, a discipline, and an art.

I enjoy laughing. I believe that laughter is a sacred sound to our God. I also believe that it has an incredible capacity to heal our bodies, our minds, and our spirits.

*Father, thank You for the sacred, healing sound of laughter.*

*The word of the Lord came to me: "Son of man,
you are living among a rebellious people. They
have eyes to see but do not see and ears to hear
but do not hear, for they are a rebellious people."
Ezekiel 12:1, 2*

Life really is fun, if we only give it a
chance. Countless moments of serendipity are
constantly alive to us and inviting us to participate, if we but have eyes to see, ears to hear, and
hearts to respond. Everyday life has its own hidden comedy. As John Powell said "Blessed is he
who has learned to laugh at himself, for he shall
never cease to be entertained." When we can
laugh at ourselves and our own situations and
the life around us, it literally produces physio-
logical and chemical changes in our bodies that
bring about a greater sense of vitality, health,
and even healing.

*Save me, Lord, from the blindness of
missing the fun serendipities of life.*

᪥

*But the Jews incited the God-fearing women of
high standing and the leading men of the city.
They stirred up persecution against Paul and
Barnabas, and expelled them from their
region. . . . And the disciples were filled with
joy and with the Holy Spirit. Acts 13:50, 52*

Pain is inevitable, but misery is optional.
We cannot avoid pain, but we can avoid joy.
God has given us such immense freedom that
He will allow us to be as miserable as we want
to be.

I know some people who spend their entire
lives practicing being unhappy, diligently pursu-
ing joylessness. They get more mileage from having people feel sorry for them than from choosing to live out their lives in the context of joy.

Joy is simple (not to be confused with easy).
At any moment in life we have at least two
options, and one of them is to choose an attitude of gratitude, a posture of grace, a commitment to joy.

᪥ ───────────────────────────

*Lord, my circumstances could dictate misery,
but I choose Your joy!*

*The seventy-two returned with joy and said,*
*"Lord, even the demons submit to us in*
*your name." Luke 10:17*

Many people agree to be joyful as soon as circumstances improve.

- As soon as the kids are grown, you'll see me shine.
- As soon as I lose weight, I'll be joyful.
- As soon as the bills get paid, as soon as, as soon as . . .

I know people who, for complex, and perhaps even justifiable, reasons have chosen to avoid the wonderful responsibility of joy in the here and now.

Joy has so much to do with how we see and hear and experience the world. It has more to do with who we are than what we have, more to do with the healthiness of our attitude than with the health of our body. Joy, above all else, is a quality that is magnified when it is shared and minimized when it is selfishly grasped.

---

*How loving You are to magnify my joy*
*as I share it with others.*

❋

*We write this to make our joy complete.*
*I John 1:4*

In our society you can buy almost anything. Security, comfort, convenience, status, and perhaps even momentary happiness can be purchased. I contend, however, that true joy has a different kind of price tag. It always has been and always will be free. We do not have to move anywhere or change anything to find it. Like grace, it is itself an inexpressible gift, available to all who would choose to partake.

But there is no such thing as cheap joy. Joy often costs pain and suffering. True joy isn't found at the end of a rainbow. It isn't captured at the top of the ladder of success. Its price tag is faithfulness, endurance, and perhaps sorrow. It has been suggested that our cup of joy can only be as deep as our cup of sorrow.

❋ _____

*You are the One who can help me choose to live in joy rather than give in to my circumstances.*

❀

*Though the fig tree does not bud and there are
no grapes on the vines . . . yet I will rejoice in
the Lord, I will be joyful in God my Savior.
Habakkuk 3:17a, 18*

The joy which I am discovering is radically
different from the kind of joy (i.e., happiness)
I've known before. Above all else, this joy does
not depend on circumstances. In fact, it is cited
most frequently in Scripture as being in spite of
circumstances.

I am beginning to realize that it isn't my
imposed limitations that hold me back as much
as my perception of those limitations. It isn't the
pain that is thwarting me as much as my attitude toward the pain. I realize that though the
difficulties are undeniably real, and will remain
so for the rest of my life, I have the opportunity
to choose a new freedom and joy if I want to.

❀ _____

*Lord, I am finding that true joy is not cheap,
but it is worth the price.*

❀

*I will lie down and sleep in peace, for you alone,*
*O Lord, make me dwell in safety. Psalm 4:8*

The word *happiness* comes from the same root as the word *happening*, suggesting that happiness is based on something happening to us. Happiness is circumstantial. If I pay off my car, I'm happy. If I get a new shirt, I'm happy. If my friends say nice things, I'm happy.

There is nothing wrong with happiness. It's wonderful. The only problem is that it's based on circumstances, and circumstances have a tendency to shift.

Joy, on the other hand, is something which defies circumstances and occurs in spite of difficult situations. Whereas happiness is a feeling, joy is an attitude. A posture. A position. A place. As Paul Sailhamer says, "Joy is that deep settled confidence that God is in control of every area of my life."

❀ ——————————— —————————————

*What a relief, God, to be reminded that*
*You are in control.*

❧

***But the fruit of the Spirit is love, joy, peace,
patience, kindness, goodness, faithfulness,
gentleness and self-control. Against such
things there is no law. Galatians 5:22, 23***

Joy is not a feeling; it is a choice. It is not
based upon circumstances; it is based upon attitude. It is free, but it is not cheap. It is the byproduct of a growing relationship with Jesus
Christ. It is a promise, not a deal. It is available
to us when we make ourselves available to Him.
It is something that we can receive by invitation
and by choice. It requires commitment, courage,
and endurance.

When Paul listed the fruit of the spirit, he
named joy second, reminding us that joy is a
very high priority in the Christian walk. A
friend once asked if it were possible that the
listing meant that joy was the second most
important virtue in the Christian faith. It's
worth considering.

❧ _____

*Today may Your Spirit be free to grow joy in mine.*

*Nehemiah said, "Go and enjoy choice food and sweet drinks, and send some to those who have nothing prepared. This day is sacred to our Lord. Do not grieve, for the joy of the Lord is your strength." Nehemiah 8:10*

During one of the most difficult times of my life, my rage to live was real, but I had, without knowing or intending it, put a lid on it by saying to myself, "When I am strong, then I'll be joyful. When the pain eases, then I'll be joyful."

The problem was reality. The pain didn't subside. And I had placed myself in the position of waiting until things got better, waiting until I knew more of God, waiting until I had enough strength to be joyful.

Through this profound and simple passage from Nehemiah, God reminded me again and again that I cannot choose to be strong, but I can choose to be joyful. And when I am willing to do that, strength will follow.

---

*Your joy, o Lord, is my strength.*

❀

*This priceless treasure we hold, so to speak, in a common earthenware jar—to show that the splendid power of it belongs to God and not to us. . . . Every day we experience something of the death of Jesus, so that we may also know the power of the life of Jesus in these bodies of ours.*
*II Corinthians 4:7, 10 (Phillips)*

I tend to avoid books with the word *victorious* in the title. Somehow they don't seem to speak to where I am. My journey just isn't described in such simple terms. I've struggled with the fact that I am unambiguously Christian and at the same time, unmistakably human. In fact, my journey has become more human, not less, since I encountered this one called Christ.

But I've discovered a new and different kind of joy that I never knew existed—a joy that can coexist with uncertainty and doubt, pain, confusion, and ambiguity—and just plain being human.

❀ ───────────────────────────

*It still amazes me, God, that You would take the common clay of me and use it for Your glory!*

*Where there is no vision, the people perish.*
*Proverbs 29:18a (KJV)*

Most of us, even in our most difficult situations, have everything we are looking for—if we would but choose to accept it and embrace it. Most of us already are in the place where God wants us to be—if we were but willing to deepen our roots, increase our courage, and expand our vision and hope.

I believe the purpose of difficulties is to help us truly discover, at a level we can only know by painful experience, the real meaning of JOY. This joy then sets us free for a new and more powerful kind of service. And this service helps us to understand, perhaps as we would never have been able to otherwise, what it really means to know God.

---

*Let me experience Your joy, Lord, that I may*
*be set free to serve You with power.*

❖

*You turned my wailing into dancing; you*
*removed my sackcloth and clothed me with joy.*
**Psalm 30:11**

There is a direct relationship between joy and strength. When the Enemy wants to rob us of our strength, the first thing he will try to take away is our joy. Nehemiah 8:10 says that "the joy of the Lord is our strength." This implies that as you choose a millimeter of joy, God will give you an inch of strength, and that gives you the capacity to choose more joy. In return, the joy gives you the capacity to gain more strength. It is a process of continual choice, and continual empowering. As cycles go, this one is blessed indeed.

❖ ───────────────────────────────

*Thank You, my Father, because just a millimeter of*
*Your joy can see me through anything today.*

✦

*A cheerful heart is good medicine, but a crushed spirit dries up the bones. Proverbs 17:22*

It was a genesis moment when I discovered that I was in control of my pain, my future, my attitudes, my life.

Norman Cousins's *Anatomy of an Illness* emphasizes both the importance of accepting responsibility for our own health and—strangely enough—the vital importance of laughter, which, Cousins believes, releases endorphins, the natural painkiller produced by our bodies.

It has long been recognized that negative attitudes such as worry can produce negative physical effects, such as ulcers. Cousins simply surmised that the opposite might also be true—that positive emotions, such as laughter and joy, would produce positive chemical reactions in the body. A cheerful heart is truly good medicine.

✦ _____

*Lord, You cheer my heart with the reassurance of Your presence.*

# THE
# COURAGE
# OF
# COMMITMENT

11/1/08

❋

*Be watchful, stand firm in your faith, be
courageous, be strong. I Corinthians 16:13 (RSV)*

To assume is to think that you already
know. Moses assumed that God couldn't use
someone who stuttered and almost detoured
one of the greatest events of the Old Testament.
Elijah assumed that he was the only believer
left. The people around David assumed that a
young boy with no armor didn't stand a chance
against a nine-foot giant. (Fortunately, David
didn't make the same assumption!) Gideon
assumed he wasn't a warrior and couldn't do
what God called him to do.

When we look only on the surface of things,
we might assume that we, too, are not ready for
a life of courage and commitment. But God
knows differently.

❋ ─────────────────────────────────

*Strengthen me, Lord. Help me to face today with
courage and commitment to whatever
You have waiting for me.*

❀

*This is how we know what love is: Jesus Christ laid down his life for us. And we ought to lay down our lives for our brothers. . . . Dear children, let us not love with words or tongue but with actions and in truth. I John 3:16, 18*

The more we genuinely seek to be authentic servant-leaders in Christ, the more we will seek out and solve problems in order to set people free.

This is serious business, but it does not necessarily have to be somber. For example, a woman I met, and her husband, spent an afternoon with Mother Teresa. Her husband has a delightful sense of humor, and Mother Teresa is known for her contagious joy. As they were getting ready to leave, the man couldn't resist asking, "Mother Teresa, what do you want to be when you grow up?" She smiled and said, "Well, I always wanted to be a stewardess."

*Unless life is lived for others, it is not worthwhile. MOTHER TERESA*

❀ ──────────────────────────

*Jesus, show me how to love from a servant heart with actions and in truth.*

1|3|08

*What good will it be for a man if he gains the whole world, yet forfeits his soul? Or what can a man give in exchange for his soul?*
*Matthew 16:26*

On her deathbed, Gertrude Stein is said to have been asked, "What is the answer?" Then after a long silence, she said, "What is the question?"

The Bible could be looked at as a Book of questions.

- Am I my brother's keeper? (Gen. 4:9)
- If God be for us, who can be against us? (Rom. 8:31)
- What is truth? (John 18:38)
- How can a man be born when he is old? (John 3:4)
- What does man gain from all his labor at which he toils under the sun? (Eccl. 1:3)
- Where can I go from your Spirit? (Ps. 139:7)
- Who is my neighbor? (Luke 10:29)
- What must I do to inherit eternal life? (Luke 10:25)

*Help me to take an honest look at my priorities and to hear Your hard questions.*

1/4/08

❧

*He has showed you, O man, what is good.*
*And what does the Lord require of you? To*
*act justly and to love mercy and to walk*
*humbly with your God. Micah 6:8*

Einstein said that imagination is more important than knowledge. Our imagination is sometimes best expressed by the quality, the boldness, and even the unpredictability and innovativeness of our questions. Try these out:

- What is the nicest compliment you've ever received?
- If you could describe your life in five words, what would they be?
- What are three things that always bring a smile to your face?
- What three things frustrate you most?
- If you could change two things about your life, what would they be?
- What are two things you want from God?
- What are two things you think God wants from you?

❧

*What are You asking me, today, God?*
*What do You want from me?*

1|8|08

❦

*[Elijah] replied, "I have been very zealous for
the Lord God Almighty. The Israelites have
rejected your covenant, broken down your altars,
and put your prophets to death with the sword.
I am the only one left, and now they are
trying to kill me too." I Kings 19:10*

One of the most common reasons why
we say *I can't* is our fear of failure. Ironically, our
most important learning experiences often
result from failure. "One of the reasons why
mature people stop growing and learning," says
John Gardner, "is that they become less and less
willing to risk failure."

Most of what we call wisdom and experience
is based on learning from our failures. Faith, it is
said, makes life possible—it does not make it
easy. Most successes are built on a foundation of
many failures. If you are to grow as a problem
solver, you must learn to "fail successfully."

❦ ———————————————————

*I hate to fail, God. Do Your work in me and make
me willing to risk failure in obedience to You.*

1-14-08

❧

*Everyone who believes that Jesus is the Christ is born of God, and everyone who loves the father loves his child as well. I John 5:1*

I Corinthians 13 is a pattern for how we're supposed to love other people—and ourselves as well. Those passages say when we love someone, we will always expect the best of them and will always stand our ground protecting them. Think about that! God really does love us like this.

Therefore, let us love ourselves as God loves us. When we do, we will see the amazing changes such an attitude brings into our lives. When we see ourselves and our problems through God's eyes, we become willing to let go of our stunted images and preconceptions.

❧ ───────────────────────────

*Heavenly Father, may Your love permeate my soul that I might love others— and even myself—as You do.*

1/15/08

❁

*Jesus answered, "I am the way and the truth and the life. No one comes to the Father except through me." John 14:6*

I have been lost on more than one occasion in the wilderness. In that situation, given the choice between someone who says, "I'll tell you the way," versus someone who says, "I will go with you," I would always choose the latter. It's always best to travel with someone who knows the way.

Jesus was called The Way, not the destination. It's a journey . . . one step at a time.

Sometimes I simply freeze my thoughts and ideas because I'm afraid to make a mistake. I have to be reminded that if you don't get lost once in a while, you're not really exploring. If you're not making mistakes, you are simply not risking enough.

❁ —————————————————————

*I want to learn to explore life with You, Jesus—failures and all.*

*1-18-08*

❀

*As Jesus and his disciples were on their way, he came to a village where a woman named Martha opened her home to him. She had a sister called Mary, who sat at the Lord's feet listening to what he said. Luke 10:38, 39*

Communication involves much more than words. One authority said that only 7 percent of our communication involves spoken words, another 38 percent is conveyed by body language including gestures and facial expressions, and 55 percent by the tone of our voice.

Listening is the most profound way you demonstrate to others that you love them. Paul Tournier said, "It is impossible to overemphasize the immense need humans have to be really listened to, to be taken seriously, to be understood. No one can develop freely in this world and find the life full, without feeling understood by at least one person."

❀ ─────────────────────────────

*Father, teach me to listen to others with full attention. Teach me to really hear what people are saying—with their whole persons, not just their words.*

*1-22-08*

❀

*For he gives us comfort in our trials so that we
in turn may be able to give the same sort of
strong sympathy to others in theirs.*
**II Corinthians 1:4 (Phillips)**

Josie is an agoraphobic—afraid of being in
open spaces—and has been trapped in her
house for decades. Her loneliness, however, has
been appeased by a woman who has phoned
her every day for the past twenty-five years.
Even when Ruth was in the hospital for knee
surgery, she made her daily phone call to Josie.
When Ruth lost her husband of forty-nine
years she continued to reach out to Josie and so
appeased her own loneliness as well.

Ruth is my mother. When I asked her about
Josie, she lit up with the joy that can only be
known through giving. Two people, two lives,
two cups of loneliness filled through the act of
one person giving without measure to another.

❀ ───────────────────────────

*Lord, who might be waiting out there to share with
me in Your encouragement?*

*Keep on loving each other as brothers.*
*Do not forget to entertain strangers, for by*
*so doing some people have entertained angels*
*without knowing it. Hebrews 13:1, 2*

I once heard a speaker say that three of the biggest handicaps in life are beauty, success, and intelligence. If I understood what he was saying, one can be handicapped by beauty in that it makes a person self-conscious, always wondering what people think and thus imprisoning the self and disabling the soul from the freedom to grow and to move.

Too much intelligence, beauty, or success can hurt us by turning us inward, so that we are forever focusing on our own wrinkled and puny soul. Both joy and depth of character come from reaching out to others.

*Liberate my puny, wrinkled soul, Lord, from constantly turning inward in self-conscious concern.*

❧

*We love because he first loved us.*
*I John 4:19*

The handicap in beauty, intelligence, or success comes when we spend our whole lives trying to make ourselves lovable rather than being committed to loving. When love finally comes, we devour it so ferociously that we can't even taste it or experience it.

There is a better way. There is a more healthy sequence for our seeking of love and attention.

God loves us, and we must let Him do so lavishly.

Therefore, we are set free to love Him, to love others, and to love ourselves.

And then, because love is like a boomerang, the wholeness of love we seek can come to us.

❧ _____

*Thank You for Your love, God, which makes it possible for me to love others and experience a full circle of love.*

❈

*Love each other with brotherly affection and*
*take delight in honoring each other.*
**Romans 12:10 (TLB)**

Feeling unloved? If you are simply waiting
for everybody else to love you, that's exactly
what you will find in return—everybody waiting for you to love them.

Mirrors and windows are both made of glass,
but they serve two distinctly different purposes.
A window allows you to see out, to see the
world, to see others, to get a perspective on life.
A mirror focuses on your preoccupation with
yourself. What we have got to do is to change
our mirrors to windows.

❈ ——————————————————

*Forgive my preoccupation with myself.*
*Change my mirrors to windows.*

*You are the world's seasoning, to make it tolerable. If you lose your flavor, what will happen to the world? And you yourselves will be thrown out and trampled underfoot as worthless. You are the world's light—a city on a hill, glowing in the night for all to see. Don't hide your light! Let it shine for all; let your good deeds glow for all to see, so that they will praise your heavenly Father.*
*Matthew 5:13-16 (TLB)*

After the church service, a little girl asked her mother, "Is it true, like the minister said, that God is bigger than we are?"

The mother responded that it was indeed true.

"He said that God lives inside of us. Is that true, Mommy?"

Again the mother replied, "Yes."

"Well, then," said the girl, "if God is bigger than us and He lives inside of us, shouldn't some of Him show through?"

Is God showing through in your life these days?

_____

*Leak through, shine through, flow through, season the world with Yourself through me, oh Lover of the world.*

❈

*Yet every advantage that I had gained I considered lost for Christ's sake. Yes, and I look upon everything as loss compared with the overwhelming gain of knowing Christ Jesus my Lord. Philippians 3:8a (Phillips)*

Perhaps one reason we fall into loneliness and despair is that we are so preoccupied with ourselves, so invested in our own egos. We're so concerned with how we are doing that we can't seem to get a clear focus on what God is doing in us and around us.

Thomas Merton said, "When humility delivers a man from attachment to his own works and his own reputation, he discovers that true joy is only possible when we have completely forgotten ourselves. And it is only when we pay no more attention to our own life and our own reputation and our own excellence that we are at last completely free to serve God for His sake alone."

❈ ────────────────────

*I am so far from the place where self is forgotten and knowing and serving You is my total focus. Be patient with me, Lord, and bring me nearer.*

❧

*But each of you must be quick to listen, slow to speak, and slow to be angry. James 1:19b (NEB)*

One of the best ways to show God's love is by listening.

In the early '70s we had an assistant instructor in Summit who was not gifted in mountaineering skills. Marcie couldn't climb that well. She frequently got lost. When it came to the technical side of mountaineering she usually went blank. She wasn't very fast or very strong. Yet when the senior instructors chose assistant instructors they were always fighting over who got Marcie. Why did everyone want her in their group? Because Marcie was a profound listener. Whenever Marcie was on a course, lives were changed dramatically because she took time to listen.

Marcie had discovered that listening and love are almost synonymous.

❧ _____

*When someone gives me their total attention, it is a gift, Lord. Help me to learn how to listen like that.*

❁

*The Lord delights in the steps of the man whose way he has made firm. Psalm 37:23*

The Serenity Prayer ("God grant me the serenity to accept the things I cannot change, the courage to change the things I can, and the wisdom to know the difference") has been around so long that we overlook its timeless wisdom and insight. Recently I came across a variation of this prayer.

"God grant me the serenity to accept the person I cannot change, the courage to change the person I can, and the wisdom to know that I am that person." In truth, the only person we can ever change is ourselves.

❁ ───────────────────────────────

*In Your great plan, You created me a unique individual, God. But thank You that You will give me courage to change certain parts of me that were not in that plan.*

❧

*Therefore encourage one another and build each*
*other up, just as in fact you are doing.*
*I Thessalonians 5:11*

There are four things that geese have to
teach us.

One, they rotate their leadership. When the
lead goose gets tired, he rotates back in the
wing and another goose flies point.

Second, by flying in a V-formation, the whole
flock gets seventy-one percent greater flying
range than if each bird flew on its own.

Third, when a goose gets sick or is wounded,
two geese fall out of formation and follow him
down to help and protect him.

Finally, it's the geese in the back who honk,
letting the leaders know that they're following
and all is well. If people thought we would be
constantly honking encouragement to them, our
churches would have standing room only.

❧ _____

*Oh God, help me to remember to*
*encourage rather than criticize.*

*But the Jews were jealous; so they rounded up some bad characters from the marketplace, formed a mob and started a riot in the city. They rushed to Jason's house in search of Paul and Silas in order to bring them out to the crowd.*
*Acts 17:5*

We have a kingdom of upside-down values and a King who didn't conform. The irony is that His followers spend most of their time and energy trying to turn things right side up to make them more respectable and acceptable. We encourage people to be more careful and sensible. We would turn them right side up and teach them to be proper believers. A pastor, in a moment of great but painful insight, said, "Isn't it curious that wherever St. Paul went there was a riot . . . but wherever I go there is a tea party?"

---

*If it will further Your kingdom, turn me upside down and inside out, oh nonconforming Jesus.*

*He put a new song in my mouth, a hymn of praise to our God. Many will see and fear, and put their trust in the Lord. Psalm 40:3*

Mark Speckman was born with no hands. I vividly remember the first day he came out for football. We all wondered how a guy with no hands could play football. He ended up not only being our starting middle linebacker, but in his senior year he was voted all–American. He also played the jazz trombone, basketball, and was a 3.6 student. Currently he's an outstanding coach and, when we can get him, he works as a Summit instructor. What made the difference? He decided to make life a challenge, and to tackle it all with joy. His joy is the source of his strength.

*Thank You for the courageous ones who encourage me because they accept the challenge and discover Your strength.*

✽

*And those who believed Peter were baptized—*
*about 3,000 in all! . . . A deep sense of awe was*
*on them all, and the apostles did many miracles.*
*And all the believers met together constantly and*
*shared everything with each other, selling their*
*possessions and dividing with those in need.*
*Acts 2:41, 43-45 (TLB)*

Isn't it a great irony that when the Son of God actually visited us on earth, one of the chief complaints against Him was that He wasn't religious enough? In Charles Sheldon's book, *In His Steps*, a pastor challenges his people to live by the simple question, "What would Jesus do?" In doing so they turn a whole town upside down with the extraordinary love of Christ.

The Book of Acts likewise describes a group of men and women who were turned inside out and upside down. The impact of their simple undeviating commitment is still affecting the world.

✽ ───────────────────────────

*Lord, I'm no Peter, but are there ways that You*
*could change my corner of the world through me?*

*But the Lord said to Samuel, "Do not consider his appearance or his height, for I have rejected him. The Lord does not look at the things man looks at. Man looks at the outward appearance, but the Lord looks at the heart." I Samuel 16:7*

The first time I ate rattlesnake meat was with Shelton Chow at his mom's restaurant. We had decided early on to be "blood brothers." So Shelton invited me to the special "family only" dinner at the restaurant, even though that made me the only person there who wasn't Chinese.

Shelton was color-blind. There was nothing wrong with his eyes of course. He just refused to make a big deal about a person's color and nationality. He invited me to play in his all-Chinese basketball league, saying, when he introduced me to the group, "This is my blood brother." They let me play the whole season.

Shelton looked at people the way God does—from the inside out.

_____

*Prejudice sneaks in, Lord. Point it out to me, and then help me see all people through Your eyes.*

*So if the Son sets you free, you will
be free indeed. John 8:36*

Are there no more frontiers for the church? Is there no wilderness? No wildness? Perhaps the freedom that Christ wanted to give us has been dammed up, detoured, and ultimately tamed. Without knowing it, we have denounced risky people as outlaws and openly forced them outside our boundaries with barbed-wire fences. And sometimes our sterile sanctuaries are shocking reminders of the power of unacceptance. We don't need "fasten your seat belts" signs in our pews because we no longer fly. We're like a group of pigeons attending meetings every Sunday where we talk passionately about flying—and then get up and walk home! Is it too costly to feel the anger, the compassion, and the loneliness that Jesus did?

*Unleash my passion for following You,
whatever that means, Jesus.*

❈

*The Christ you have to deal with is not a weak person outside you, but a tremendous power inside you. II Corinthians 13:3b (Phillips)*

Vance Havner said, "The great tragedy today is that the situation is desperate, but the saints are not." What an irony for an organization that is based on the unconditional love of the wounded Christ. We are understocked with people who feel real feelings and express them. If the passionate resurrected Christ truly lives within us, then shouldn't some of His feelings for a desperate world show through?

As my good friend Jim Wilson says: "If you really understand that salvation calls us to a passionate interaction with a hurting world, then perhaps instead of being bored to tears, you would be moved to them."

❈ _____

*Help me to get in touch with Your power within me, and move me to interaction with this hurting world.*

❧

*The Lord is my strength and my song; he has become my salvation. Psalm 118:14*

In my sterile search for success, I have sometimes chosen to be effective rather than committed. I have chosen to be successful rather than merely being faithful. Sometimes my calendar is full, but my heart is empty. The Lord tries to fill my cup, but I poke a hole in it. Perforated trust.

Am I afraid to trust Him completely? Am I afraid to love others without knowing whether or not I'll be loved in return? I still don't understand His kind of love—a love which expects nothing.

As Ian Thomas says, God doesn't ask us to be sensational—He simply asks us to be a miracle. A miracle is something that cannot be explained apart from Jesus Christ. He wants to borrow our humanity to communicate His truths to the world. He doesn't give us His strength; He is our strength.

❧ ─────────────────────────────────

*In Your strength, Lord, help me to communicate You to the world.*

❈

*Then he said to them all: "If anyone would come after me, he must deny himself and take up his cross daily and follow me." Luke 9:23*

Christ frequently asked people to do difficult things. To the paralytic He said, "Pick up your bed and walk." To Peter He said, "Drop your nets. Leave them behind and follow Me." He encourages us to love our enemies; to lose our lives in order to find them; to pick up our crosses daily and follow Him. His love is not a wimpy love. It is a "hard-nosed agape."

What is He saying to you today? What areas of your life are not conformed to His image? He became like us so that we could become more like Him.

❈ _____

*What are You saying to me, Christ of the Cross? What does it mean for me to take up my cross today?*

❄️

*Now to him who is able to do immeasurably more than all we ask or imagine, according to his power that is at work within us, to him be glory in the church and in Christ Jesus throughout all generations, for ever and ever! Amen.*
*Ephesians 3:20, 21*

To solve some of the problems of hunger, loneliness, war, stress, and boredom in our incredibly complex future, it will take more than a little bit of creativity.

Creativity doesn't take genius as much as it takes exercise. We are all endowed with a remarkable, 17-percent water-based, analog, electrochemical, digital, quintrasensing, servo-mechanism computer, otherwise known as a brain, that can do astonishing things. Like any gift we've been given we must use it; we must exercise it in order to grow. Teddy Roosevelt said, "Do what you can, with what you have, where you are."

❄️ ⎯⎯⎯⎯⎯⎯⎯⎯⎯⎯⎯⎯⎯⎯⎯⎯⎯⎯⎯

*Thank You for Your power within. Spark my creativity to combine with that power, and accomplish Your purposes through me.*

❧

*But seek first his kingdom and his righteousness,*
*and all these things will be given to you as well.*
*Matthew 6:33*

When he was in college, Chris had numerous problems. One evening he discussed his problems with a great deal of intricacy and emotion with an older friend, Dave.

Then Dave picked up a Bible and read Matt. 6:33. Chris thanked him and began elaborating again on each of his problems.

Once more Dave picked up the Scripture and read Matt. 6:33. Chris became impatient and said something like, "Yeah, yeah, okay, that's great. Now, regarding the college situation . . ." Again Dave read Matt. 6:33. Chris finally left. For the next three days he smoldered. Finally, however, it dawned on him how this "simple" verse could place his problems in a whole new light.

❧ ────────────────────────────

*Help me to live today with my focus on seeking Your*
*kingdom and Your righteousness.*

❁

*Love is patient, love is kind. It does not envy,
it does not boast, it is not proud.
I Corinthians 13:4*

Both Jesus and Paul were characterized by simplicity. Their intention was not to confuse or deceive but to clarify and illuminate. Paul was not always easy to understand, nor was Jesus.

*Simplicity* does not necessarily mean easy to understand. *Simple* means there are no hidden or double meanings. Simple is saying what you mean. As Albert Day said, "Where there's simplicity words can be taken at face value. One says what one means and means what one says."

Where there's simplicity there is no artificiality. One does not try to appear younger or wiser or richer than one is. Or more saintly.

❁ ─────────────────────────────

*Jesus, You know me—the real me. Teach me to live
without artificiality, with Your simplicity.*

*Now I want you to know, brothers, that what has happened to me has really served to advance the gospel. Philippians 1:12*

When Sherry Leonard was young, she contracted muscular dystrophy. At one point in her life, her despair was so deep that she contemplated suicide. After she encountered Jesus Christ, she realized she had a choice about what her outlook would be.

As we returned from a challenging wilderness experience for the physically disabled, she said, "Muscular dystrophy is my gift from God." It gives her the opportunity to share her relationship with Jesus Christ. I was humbled to think of the many times I have complained about some of the paltry problems and pains that I've had to endure. Sherry's joy is radiant even though she will never be able to walk, even though she has to use one arm to lift the other. Her zest for life and God is contagious.

*Thank You, God, for the people in my life who model commitment to You.*

❧

*Not that I have already obtained all this, or have already been made perfect, but I press on to take hold of that for which Christ Jesus took hold of me. Philippians 3:12*

Somebody once said that "perfectionism leads to procrastination, and procrastination in turn leads to paralysis." It is true that we must pursue excellence. But we must also avoid that nagging tendency to strive for perfection, especially on the first attempt at a task.

Babe Ruth struck out 1,330 times, yet was considered one of the greatest baseball players of all time. Thomas Edison, one of this country's most famous inventors, discovered at least 1,800 ways not to make a light bulb. Columbus thought he was finding a shortcut to India. Johannes Kepler stumbled on to the idea of interplanetary gravity because of assumptions which were right for the wrong reasons.

---

*Lord, make me aware when my perfectionism is paralyzing me and keeping me from pressing on.*

❧

*Your love has given me great joy and encouragement, because you, brother, have refreshed the hearts of the saints. Philemon 7*

Have you ever spent time with someone who could give you ninety-three reasons why a problem can't be solved? Have you ever been around someone who has all sorts of elaborate methods for justifying why the situation is impossible?

Lack of encouragement and ingratitude seem to go together. People who are truly thankful for life will usually be supportive and encouraging. The word *encouragement* means "to put courage into," and since life is often notoriously difficult, we need all the encouragement we can get. Author Jean Houston says, "Perhaps encouragement is the greatest and single most powerful gift that God has ever given us. Nothing seems to impact our lives as much as encouragement."

❧ ————————————————————

*Father God, how thankful I am for the people who have encouraged me. Help me to give that gift to someone today.*

❀

*You did not choose me, but I chose you and appointed you to go and bear fruit—fruit that will last. Then the Father will give you whatever you ask in my name.*
*John 15:16*

Christianity is not like a football game where only eleven can play at a time while the rest of us watch. Too many of us are on the sidelines. Too many of us are on the shelf indefinitely preparing to get involved. Many of us claim that we would be involved if only there were more opportunities.

Oswald Chambers hit the nail on the head when he said, "Looking for opportunities to serve God is an impertinence; every time and all the time is our opportunity to serve God. God does not expect us to work for Him but with Him."

"Someday," says Teilhard de Chardin, "after mastering the winds, the waves, the tides, and gravity, we shall harness for God the energies of love and then, for the second time in the history of the world, man will have discovered fire."

❀ ————————————————————————

*Oh God, fire up Your love within and work through me today.*

*For God has not given us a spirit of fear, but a*
*spirit of power and love and a sound mind.*
*II Timothy 1:7 (Phillips)*

Journalist Hunter Thompson said, "Most writers tend to sit on the sidelines away from the action, detached from any sort of involvement and write as a mere spectator or observer, as to what is going on." He recommended what he called Gonzo Journalism where the journalist would jump into the middle of the fray, and, amidst all the difficulties, pains, and joys, write from the view of a participant rather than that of a spectator.

Likewise, "Gonzo Christianity" means we are no longer passive observers, but active participants of life, jumping into the needs of the world through the power of the Holy Spirit.

*You are calling me to get involved with the hurts*
*and needs around me. There are so many,*
*Lord. Where do I begin?*

❧

*I will instruct you and teach you in the way you should go; I will counsel you and watch over you.*
**Psalm 32:8**

Gonzo Christianity is the willingness to be involved, the willingness to be open to God's leadership. It is the willingness to be used by God for His purposes here and now and usually in such simple ways. As Mother Teresa says, "We can do no great things; only small things with great love."

Compassion is not necessarily quantitative. Several years ago World Vision developed a wonderful poster which said in big bold letters across the top, *How Do You Feed a Hungry World*? In the bottom right-hand corner was a tiny picture of a child and these words in small type: *One at a Time.*

Set out to conquer the world by conquering your problems one at a time with Christ at your side.

Go with peace and assurance that there is no problem you and Christ cannot handle together.

❧ _____

*You have not left me to solve my problems alone.*
*I go with the confidence of Your counsel.*

※

*I know your deeds, that you are neither cold nor hot. I wish you were either one or the other! So, because you are lukewarm—neither hot nor cold—I am about to spit you out of my mouth.*
*Revelation 3:15, 16*

Tragically some Christians are more committed to petty piety than risking following the living unpredictable Jesus Christ. Some still prefer a religion filled with soft light through stained-glass windows and quiet organ music, safe and undemanding rules, and a few emotional quivers. Chad Walsh once said, "I suspect that the enemy has called off his attempt to convert these people to agnosticism. After all," he says, "if a man travels far enough away from real Christianity, he is liable to see it in perspective and decide it's really true. It is much safer from Satan's point of view to vaccinate a man with a mild case of Christianity so as to protect him from the real disease." Ouch!

※ _____

*Don't let me become lukewarm, Jesus. Rekindle the fire of my commitment to You.*

❧

*Whoever serves me must follow me; and where I am, my servant also will be. My Father will honor the one who serves me. John 12:26*

The more we genuinely seek to be an authentic servant-leader in Christ, the more we will seek out and solve problems in order to set people free.

In other words, God's love sets us free from the many struggles we all wrestle with in order to allow us to be fully free to love others. And love will always find a way to be practical. To love often means to solve problems. Love's problems may be as simple as mowing someone's lawn or as complicated as trying to find ways to solve world hunger.

We are called to joyful, competent, compassionate servanthood in the world. This is difficult but not impossible. It is challenging but not beyond what God wants to do and can do in our lives.

❧ _____

*Show me love's problems that I may be Your joyful, compassionate servant.*

❀

*We are therefore Christ's ambassadors, as though*
*God were making his appeal through us.*
*II Corinthians 5:20a*

I wish I could blow every dusty, safe
image of the Christian faith from your mind.
We are living expressions of the living Christ.
He said that we were called to do even greater
things than He did. We're called to a life of
action, of incarnation, called to re–present Jesus
in a world continually, not just represent Him.
Not just be His ambassadors, but re–present
Him. That is plan A.

We may look at each other and roll our eyes
and ask, "What's plan B?" But there is no plan
B. Watching our fumbling, faltering humanity,
God said, "Yes, this is the way I want to continue to express My incarnation in the world. I
want to continue to reveal My Son through
these people called "Christ–ones."

❀ ──────────────────────────

*Re–present Your Son through my life, God.*
*Forgive me for taking so lightly my call to be a*
*"Christ–one."*

❀

*In the beginning was the Word, and the Word
was with God, and the Word was God. . . .
The Word became flesh and lived for a while
among us. John 1:1, 14a (RSV)*

Our theology must become biography, not
only because the world needs it so desperately,
but also because that was the supreme example
God gave us in Christ. The Incarnation . . .

The Incarnation gives us an ultimate model.
If God had wanted to teach us psychology, He'd
have sent us a psychologist; if He had wanted to
teach us about science, He'd have sent a scien-
tist. But He wanted to teach us about person-
hood, so He sent a Person, the Word made
flesh—not only to show us what God is like,
but also what life is like. . . .

God revealed Himself through a life-style,
becoming flesh, matter, substance, real. Hence,
God works in the eternal present, through us
here and now.

❀ ───────────────────────────────

*Use my person to incarnate Your love, God. Help
me be willing to let the world see You through me.*

***My command is this: Love each other as I have loved you. John 15:12***

The older I get the more dignity, elegance, and power I see in simplicity. I am discovering that the truly deep people have at the core of their being the genius of being simple.

To look at Jesus, to understand from the gospels how He lived, and live by the commands He gave us is not very complicated. "Love your neighbor as yourself," "love God with all your heart, soul, and mind," "as I have loved you, so you must love one another"—it's really pretty straightforward. In fact, it's simple! But it isn't easy.

*Jesus, Your simple message of love is clear, but how often I complicate it.*

❄

*I leave the past behind and with hands out-*
*stretched to whatever lies ahead I go straight for*
*the goal. Philippians 3:14 (Phillips)*

We could see for miles as we slowly tack-
led one of the toughest rock climbs in the
Sierras. "The Prow" was 800 feet of sheer rock,
and when you rappelled off the top to a small
ledge 150 feet below, you felt as though you had
jumped off a ten-story building. It's a scary
experience for anyone, and today Sherry was
trying it for the first time. Because of muscular
dystrophy, Sherry couldn't walk, but she was
determined to learn to climb mountains! With
the help of the Summit staff, she was now
doing what no other disabled person had ever
done—she was rappelling off "The Prow,"
laughing all the way down.

Sherry had found in God the courage to love
herself as she is and live life as fully as possible.

❄ _____

*I'm tired of saying, "I can't," Lord. Help me to*
*courageously go straight for the goal.*

***I have declared to both Jews and Greeks that they must turn to God in repentance and have faith in our Lord Jesus. Acts 20:21***

In the Los Angeles airport with my sons, Josh and Zac, I spotted Bob Wieland in a crowd of travelers. "C'mon guys," I said, "here's someone you have to meet."

It's not every day that you get to meet someone who's walked across America—on his hands! In Vietnam Bob stepped on a hidden bomb that blew off both his legs. When Bob recovered from the accident he began training, lifting weights to strengthen his body. It took him 4.9 million "steps" to walk across America, swinging his body along on his hands, wearing thickly padded gloves. He started at Knotts Berry Farm in California and almost four years later, he ended up at the Vietnam War Memorial in Washington D.C.

Why did he do it? "To encourage those with legs to take the first step in faith to please God."

*Father, use me in my unique situation to encourage others to step out in faith.*

❈

*What I want from you is your true thanks;*
*I want your promises fulfilled. I want you to*
*trust me in your times of trouble, so I can*
*rescue you, and you can give me glory.*
**Psalm 50:14, 15 (TLB)**

D r. Ken Campbell is no ordinary dentist. For one thing, he doesn't look ordinary. Because he was burned very badly in a car crash several years ago, he has no eyebrows, and the skin around his eyes and mouth is pulled back tight. The burns were so painful that Ken prayed he would die. But God had other plans for him, and that's another reason Ken isn't an ordinary dentist.

Ken decided to not give up. Now he sees dentistry as an opportunity to witness for Christ. And he's found his life further enriched with trips to Central America where he gives free dental help to people who couldn't get it otherwise.

❈ _____

*Help me to see ways, God, that my life*
*can be lived for Your glory.*

❧❧

*You will surely forget your trouble, recalling it only as waters gone by. Life will be brighter than noonday, and darkness will become like morning.*
*Job 11:16, 17*

I hated to climb out of my warm sleeping bag that morning in the Sierra Nevadas. It's always hard to move in the morning, and I was feeling sorry for myself until I saw Tim Burton begin to struggle out of his sleeping bag.

Tim was working as a carpenter when he fell off a platform and hit his head. Since that time he has not been able to walk, and has trouble moving and even talking. It took Tim half an hour to get out of his sleeping bag, but he kept at it. When he was finally out, he looked over at me and said in his stammering voice, "Ok-k-kay, Tim. I'm r-r-ready f-for a-a-a-anything!"

Later, as he struggled up the side of the mountain with the help of two instructors, he kept saying, "Oh, W-W-Wow!" We named the climb *Oh, Wow!* after Tim Burton.

❧❧ _____

*Oh God, You give me hope in the midst of my worst troubles.*

❧

*Satisfy us in the morning with your unfailing love, that we may sing for joy and be glad all our days. Make us glad for as many days as you have afflicted us, for as many years as we have seen trouble. Psalm 90:14, 15*

A friend of mine was born with a serious handicap. She also lives with the life-long scar of being sexually abused as a child. Because her parents died when she was eighteen, she is alone in the world with her incessant pain and dreadful memories. I can't tell her of a seven-step process for fixing her problems. All I can do is listen when she wants to talk about her hurts, cry with her when she weeps, and pray that God will grant her a few incandescent moments of joy to carry her through the years ahead.

"Life is more difficult than I thought," a friend said recently. "Reality, for the most part, cannot simply be altered to suit our convenience or circumstances."

❧ ───────────────────────────

*I praise You that Your unfailing love carries me through whatever life includes.*

*I thank my God in all my remembrance of
you. . . . It is right for me to feel thus about
you all, because I hold you in my heart.*
*Philippians 1:3, 7a (RSV)*

God often sends us special people for certain times. For me, Don and Jacque Anderson were two genuine examples of what the Christian life is supposed to be about.

When I first met them, I was a struggling Young Life leader living on $200 a month. Don and Jacque gave me a room above their garage and welcomed me into their family.

Although they both worked full time, their home seemed to me to be a genuine extension of the church. (I still remember vividly the night 120 wild and wonderful high-school kids jammed every corner of the Andersons' living room.) Their kitchen was a place for anyone who was hurting or struggling to receive comfort. Their home was filled not only with their own joy but also with that of Christ.

*My heart is full of gratitude, God, for the special
people You have sent through my life.*

❧

*Because you know that the testing of your faith develops perseverance. Perseverance must finish its work so that you may be mature and complete, not lacking anything. James 1:3, 4*

Ken Taylor is a walking, breathing model of perseverance! He started *The Living Bible* project to provide an easy-to-understand version of the Bible for his large family. In his excitement over what he had produced, he sought out a publisher, but over the months, dozens of publishers turned him down. Still determined to see his work published, Taylor used his savings to publish it himself.

During the first year, his *Living Letters* sold only eight hundred copies. But Ken Taylor refused to give up. Today, *The Living Bible* has sold more than 39 million copies, has been translated into countless languages, and has touched more lives for Christ than he ever imagined possible.

❧ ─────────────────────────────

*Teach me to keep going, Lord, to persevere when I want to give up.*

✹

*Whoever finds his life will lose it, and whoever loses his life for my sake will find it.*
**Matthew 10:39**

A famous preacher at a Christian rally I attended said, "You're either lost or you're lost." There was a long pause while we wondered if we had heard correctly, and then he repeated it again. "You're either lost or you're lost." Then he said, "You're either lost in the world or you're lost in Christ."

That evening he challenged us to understand what it means to lose your life to find it and what it means to be recklessly abandoned to the person of Jesus Christ. For something to have value, we must invest in it. Whether in our families, our relationship with Christ, or anywhere else in our lives, there's no such thing as a quick fix. There are no easy answers. Quality living takes time and commitment. We've got to hang in there.

✹ ————————————————

*Jesus Christ, show me what it means for me to lose my life for Your sake—to be recklessly abandoned to You.*

❧

*I am always thinking of the Lord; and because
he is so near, I never need to stumble or to fall.
Psalm 16:8 (TLB)*

I had a quiet but profound experience one
Saturday when I was asked to speak to 350
women at a luncheon. I shared the platform
with a serene woman of simple stature. Janice
Sakuma had lost her eleven-year-old daughter
to a dreaded disease. Yet in the midst of her pain
she radiated a peace that I have rarely seen or
experienced.

Her pain had driven her to the point where
she had let go, opened up her hands, and let
God fill them.

Janice in her simple, humble way showed me
what God is really like. She was simply a believer. Many Christians work and work and work
to tune their lives to the harmony of God. She
simply let go.

❧ _____

*Tune me to the harmony of Your nearness, Lord.*

❧

*Then shalt thou call, and the Lord shall answer;*
*thou shalt cry, and he shall say, Here I am.*
*Isaiah 58:9a (KJV)*

By its very nature, life has the capacity and propensity to change.

We sometimes assume that God is leading toward a prearranged goal. He may not be. What He desires most from us is obedience. Surrender to His person. Sensitivity to His presence.

Our God is a God of history and a God of the future, but He lives in the present tense. His name is *I Am*, not *I Was* or *I Will Be*. A certain kind of peace invades us when we realize that this moment is complete in and of itself. That this moment is sacred. That this moment is enough. That this moment is not lacking in anything that we need.

❧ —————————————————————

*Oh Great I Am, thank You for this present*
*moment and the reality of You in it.*

***But you will receive power when the Holy Spirit comes on you; and you will be my witnesses in Jerusalem, and in all Judea and Samaria, and to the ends of the earth. Acts 1:8***

Harvard did a study some years ago on the subject of nonverbal communication. The research revealed that there are over seven hundred thousand different ways to communicate without words. We don't just speak the message, we are the message. When we limit Christ's message to spoken words, we are not only limiting what He might do, but we are also placing ourselves under a tremendous handicap.

We are called to be His witnesses, not just to do witnessing for Him. It's not a matter of imitation as much as it is inhabitation. The Sermon on the Mount doesn't command us to act salty, but to be the earth's salt.

*Inhabit my life, oh Christ, and teach me what it means to be Your witness.*

❄

*Therefore, I urge you, brothers, in view of God's mercy, to offer your bodies as living sacrifices, holy and pleasing to God—this is your spiritual act of worship. Romans 12:1*

When God chose to reveal Himself uniquely, He did it through a person, through a life-style—because He knew then, as now, that what we are is far more potent than what we say. Two thousand years ago God declared unambiguously in the life of Jesus Christ that human flesh is a good conductor of divine electricity—and, as far as I understand, He hasn't changed His mind.

❄ _____

*It amazes me that You actually walked this earth. But, Jesus, it is both humbling and amazing to think that You still walk this earth through Your people.*

❧

*You are to be perfect, like your Heavenly Father.*
*Matthew 5:48 (Phillips)*

It was a simple carpenter who gave *Energy* not its name but its power. When He said, "Be perfect, even as your Father in heaven is perfect," he wasn't talking about the perfectionism that so many try to achieve, but rather a quality of wholeness that many have never tasted before. He asks us to be indelible rather than impeccable. He calls for a depth of maturity that bases its actions in personal self-worth more than how many records one holds. It is not a bludgeon to condemn us, but an affirmation to set us free. The key question is, "In what do I place my confidence?"

❧ _____

*Heavenly Father, I want to understand what it means for me, here and now, to be "perfectly whole."*

❈

*For it is God who works in you to will and to act according to his good purpose.*
*Philippians 2:13*

Many of us may feel frustrated because we sense our lives starting to atrophy—and we can't identify the cause. Often it is a preoccupation with work that blurs things that are truly important—my relationship to God, my health, my family, my personal growth, and my friends. Too often we buy into these myths:

- Work is the primary source of your identity.
- You are not really serving the Lord unless you push to the point of fatigue.
- The more you work, the more God loves you.
- Most of your problems would be solved if you would only work harder.
- The Bible says that the most important thing a person can do is to work.

If we, as Christians, do not demonstrate as well as speak a different reply than the world around us, then where is our message?

❈ ───────────────────────────

*May my life reflect Your message, Lord, Your purposes.*

❧

*As Jesus walked beside the Sea of Galilee, he saw Simon and his brother Andrew casting a net into the lake, for they were fishermen. "Come, follow me," Jesus said, "and I will make you fishers of men." Mark 1:16, 17*

Jesus would not have been a good promoter for the work ethic. Not only did He leave His own job as a carpenter, but He also called other people away from their jobs. He preached about the dangers of becoming preoccupied with work and the pursuit of wealth and power. He told a rich young man to sell all his possessions and give the proceeds to the poor—hardly a wise investment of capital from a businessman's viewpoint.

Early Christians put much greater emphasis on personal salvation than they did analyzing trends, making long-range projections, and worrying about budgets. Their first priority was to grow closer to God.

❧ ────────────────────────────

*Help me honestly examine my priorities, Lord. I want my first priority to be to follow You.*

✥

*Look at the birds of the air; they do not sow
or reap or store away in barns, and yet your
heavenly Father feeds them. Are you not much
more valuable than they? Matthew 6:26*

We are a nation of people consumed by
having. We want to have not only material
things, but facts. We want to have knowledge.
We want to have information. We even want to
have love and inspiration. We want to have happiness and have abundance. Ownership seems to
be the king of virtues, no matter what the commodity, and yet we are a society of notoriously
unhappy people; lonely, anxious, depressed,
dependent.

By now we should have learned that unrestricted satisfaction of all desires is not conducive to well-being. We know this to be true
for our children, and yet sometimes we fail to
recognize its truth in our own lives. Greed and
peace preclude each other.

✥ ─────────────────────────────

*I need Your grace, Heavenly Father,
to transform my need to "have."*

❧❧

*If we live like this, we shall know that we are*
*children of the truth and can reassure ourselves in*
*the sight of God, even if our own hearts make us*
*feel guilty. For God is infinitely greater than our*
*hearts, and he knows everything.*
*I John 3:19, 20 (Phillips)*

You can't heal what you can't feel. As one
of my defense mechanisms, I learned how to
think "about" feelings and talk "about" feelings
rather than really feel them. The two are galax-
ies apart. I learned that it was a mistake to
repress my feelings instead of learning how to
properly express them. Without knowing it, I
was cutting off God's ability to work in me.

Feelings are real—they need to be experienced and shared—but they are not always
accurate. We must constantly balance our feelings against the truths revealed in Scripture.

❧❧ _____

*Thank You for the gift of feelings,*
*God—all kinds of them.*

❄

*His eyes are on the ways of men;*
*he sees their every step. Job 34:21*

Patti Blumenthal does exceptional work
with kids from the probation department. These
kids have no shortage of problems and difficulties. One day when she was telling me about
her work, she kept using some initials that were
unfamiliar to me. After the third or fourth time,
my curiosity got the best of me.

"All right, Patti," I said, "what's this NTS?"

With great delight she explained, "Oh, that's
the Next Tiny Step. These kids can't take big
steps, but they can take tiny ones."

When we are overwhelmed by life we feel
lost and powerless. We feel like we are at the
mercy of others, and we constantly wait for
someone else to act. Little do we realize that
there are countless little steps that we can take.

❄ _____

*When the pressures of life surround me, Lord,*
*remind me that I need only take one step*
*at a time to get through.*

❧

*Because of your great compassion you did not abandon them in the desert. By day the pillar of cloud did not cease to guide them on their path, nor the pillar of fire by night to shine on the way they were to take. Nehemiah 9:19*

God didn't ask the Israelites to go all the way to Canaan in a day. He only asked that they take "the Next Tiny Step." This concept has had a profound impact on my life. It has been of inestimable value, especially during times of difficulty. It has helped me realize that I can always initiate some change, no matter how small.

When we have a sense of doing something, we realize that we are not paralyzed. We can still move. We can still make life happen. God doesn't ask us to take big steps . . . just the Next Tiny Step.

❧ _____

*Thank You, God, that all I need to do is take the Next Tiny Step.*

❧

*He arose and rebuked the wind, and said to the sea, "Peace, be still!" And the wind ceased and there was a great calm. Mark 4:39 (NKJV)*

In *Winning Life's Toughest Battles*, Dr. Julias Segal writes poignantly of the importance of taking action, no matter how small, in times of great stress and difficulty. The more difficult the trouble, he says, the more important it is to take some small step—to act, and, hence, reduce your feelings of hopelessness and powerlessness.

Persons traumatized by crisis often feel cut off not only from their past, but from their future as well. They become disoriented and feel lost. When one is mired in such a crisis, Segal insists that the smallest action can be the key to survival.

❧ ———————————————————

*Lord, in my difficulties You always provide room to move—at least one small step.*

❧

*As I was with Moses, so I will be with you; I will never leave you nor forsake you. . . . Have I not commanded you? Be strong and courageous. Do not be terrified; do not be discouraged, for the Lord your God will be with you wherever you go.*
*Joshua 1:5b, 9*

I recall a time in my life when I went through a trough so deep that I thought I would need a ladder just to get to the bottom. Fortunately I had some friends who walked through that valley with me. At one point, when I was ready to give up, one friend did the most surprising thing. He grabbed me by the shirt collar, shook me, and said, "Tim, less than two percent of the world's population ever gets to know life at this level. You have got to go through it. I'm not going to let you stop, and I'm not going to let you go around it. We'll go through this thing no matter how painful it is. The way out is through."

❧ _____

*Father, thank You that You promised to go with me, all the way through.*

*But when he, the Spirit of truth, comes, he will guide you into all truth. He will not speak on his own; he will speak only what he hears, and he will tell you what is yet to come.*
*John 16:13*

A map is not the same as being there. A map shows you where to go and how to get there. It shows you where the high places are and what they will be like. But it is no substitute for the wilderness itself.

The Bible is a map and a survival manual for the Christian life. The Holy Spirit is the compass and our personal guide. But we still have to put our boots on and explore the wilderness ourselves. We can't get there by taxi.

---

*Because You are my guide through the wilderness of life, oh Spirit of Truth, I can explore with confidence.*

❧

*In everything, do to others what you would have*
*them do to you, for this sums up the Law*
*and the Prophets. Matthew 7:12*

I always look forward to Ken's smile and friendly handshake. No matter how tough my day has been, he makes it seem as though the world is a friendly place. Ken works at my favorite soup-and-salad restaurant. I've watched him in his interactions with "clients," as he calls them. He is friendly, open, caring, and easy to talk to.

I mentioned that to him one night. "You are really good at what you do, Ken."

He said, "Maybe it's because of my basic loneliness. I need to reach out to people. I find that when I reach out to people, they reach back to me. In a sense, my own loneliness is a gift. It encourages me to keep reaching out to others."

The principle is as solid as the law of gravity. When I reach out to people, they in turn reach out to me.

❧

*Thank You for the way Your great principle*
*of love works, Jesus.*

✹

*O my soul, don't be discouraged. Don't be upset.*
*Expect God to act! For I know that I shall again*
*have plenty of reason to praise him for all that*
*he will do. He is my help! He is my God!*
*Psalm 42:11 (TLB)*

I heard a story about how actress Joan Blondell used to pull herself out of the dumps. She said, "I set the timer for six and a half minutes to be lonely and twenty-two minutes to feel sorry for myself. Then when the bell rings I take a shower, go for a walk or a swim, or I cook something and think about something else."

Isn't that great? Got a timer? Do something different today. Anything. Drive to work a different way. Play some different music. Rearrange your furniture. It won't cost you anything but a little creativity.

Make a three-minute commitment to joy. Thank God for five things. Right now. And keep inching along with those Next Tiny Steps.

✹ ───────────────────────────────

*I praise You, Faithful God,*
*for these five things: . . .*

❧

*"And we all hear these men telling in our own*
*languages about the mighty miracles of God!"*
*They stood there amazed and perplexed.*
*"What can this mean?" they asked each other.*
*But others in the crowd were mocking. "They're*
*drunk, that's all!" Acts 2:11b-13 (TLB)*

Sometimes I worry about us. At the most
critical time in history, we're sitting like pickles
in a jar getting preserved—safe, careful, nice
dead people. What would it be like knowing
God without having our shirts tucked in, without having our skirts pressed?

We are all pretending to look good. In a herd
we travel the well-worn paths, afraid to risk the
adventure of newness, timidly shying away from
the unknown. The Bible is crammed with
wilderness experiences—but we prefer to graze
on fenced-in land.

It is infrequent if not impossible to hear of a
church that could be described as "rowdy with
the love of God."

❧ _____

*Give me courage, Lord, to go without starch and*
*preservatives, to risk something for You today.*

*Create in me a clean heart, O God; and renew a right spirit within me. Psalm 51:10 (KJV)*

When I invited Christ into my life, I, in a sense, lit the fire. But obviously, there is more to the Christian life than one step of faith. The process continues. The colors of each season get both deeper and brighter. The second fire is the one you light as you commit yourself to a journey of excellence in Jesus Christ, when you choose to remain on the growing edge where life is more significant, and more dangerous.

It requires discipline. It also requires tenacity. The prefix *re*, meaning "again," begins to preface much of your vocabulary: rededicate, rediscover, rebound, receive, redefine, reflect, refresh, regenerate. You realize the necessity of this process, else your work becomes simply ornamental and your leisure just analgesic.

Keep on relighting the fire.

*Renew me, God. Refresh my Spirit and rejuvenate Your life within me.*

❋

*They seek me daily, and delight to know
my ways. . . . Isaiah 58:2a (KJV)*

If you can be satisfied with little, then
enough becomes a banquet. Peace is both a
process of panting after God's own heart, and
also letting him find you. Because you are
found, you are free to seek. And you find that
the God at the end of the journey is the same
one you knew at the beginning. Learning to let
life happen rediscovers the importance of small
things. It relishes childlike joys of the everyday
wonders of being alive.

Some of God's miracles are small. Some of
God's truths are quite simple. If you cannot do
great things for God, do small things in a great
way.

❋ ───────────────────────────

*Again today I seek You, God, in the small and
everyday miracles of being alive.*

✿

*Your attitude should be the same as that of Christ Jesus: Who, being in very nature God, did not consider equality with God something to be grasped, but made himself nothing, taking the very nature of a servant, being made in human likeness. And being found in appearance as a man, he humbled himself and became obedient to death—even death on a cross! Philippians 2:5–8*

The key to servanthood is to let God use you in a way that He has planned. *Let* is a potent word, a word of tremendous faith with volumes of meaning poured into it. It assumes the total, unconditional, unbelievable love and good will of the Father. It assumes that heaven is crowded with the good gifts that the Father wants to give His children. *Let* means saying, "Father, I give You permission to do so and so for us down here on earth." It is saying, "I invite You to do Your great work in even me."

✿ ————————————————————

*As Your servant, Divine Master, I invite You to do Your work in my life.*

✿

*And we pray this in order that you may live a
life worthy of the Lord and may please him in
every way: bearing fruit in every good work,
growing in the knowledge of God, being
strengthened with all power according to his
glorious might so that you may have great
endurance and patience. Colossians 1:10, 11*

What hinders you right now from
becoming the man or woman of God you
would like to be? The typical view of the
Christian life is one of deliverance from trouble.
Scripture, however, calls us to deliverance in
trouble. The difference is not just a semantic
one. It's crucial that we keep the flow of God's
Spirit active, and refuse to give in to circumstance or discouragement.

God wants to penetrate our attitudes so He
can free us up to stick our noses right into the
heart of life wherever we are.

✿ _____

*Spirit of God, flow freely through my soul, that
I may be ready to stick my nose right into
the heart of life where I am.*

❈

*No, in all these things we are more than conquerors through him who loved us. Romans 8:37*

If you want to live to the maximum, you must learn to arise early and seize the day, to immerse yourself in the heart of life rather than remaining on the periphery, insulated from any consequences. On the wall of a college workout room, I saw this statement: "A person who says he can't and a person who says he can are, strangely enough, usually both right."

God wants you to do more than merely exist. He wants you to live to the fullest. As the comic-strip philosopher Pogo said, "Gentlemen, we are surrounded by insurmountable opportunities."

❈ ———————————————————————

*Lord, usually I seem to be less than a conqueror.*
*Help me to seize the opportunities You*
*offer to live life to the fullest.*

*You are my God, and I will give you thanks; you are my God, and I will exalt you. Psalm 118:28*

Someone once said, "Success is getting what you want. Happiness is wanting what you get." The Bible expresses the same idea a different way—"Give thanks in all circumstances; for this is the will of God in Christ Jesus for you."

The essence of happiness and peace lies in gratitude. Two things I have learned: (1) gratitude is not optional for a Christian, and (2) gratitude is the source of peace.

If you would really like to change the world within you and thereby around you, learn to be diligent in thanksgiving. Gratitude can be expressed by hard work, by patience, by laughter, by creativity, by persistence, by the quality of your love, by the depth of your hope, and by the certainty of your peace.

*Oh God, my heart is full of gratitude for You for Your love for me, for the life You have given me. Praise You, God!*

# The Courage of Commitment

❀

*My times are in your hands. Psalm 31:15a*

Avoiding the present moment has almost become a habit in our society. For the major part of our working lives we are taught to sacrifice the present for the future. When the future arrives, it becomes the present, and we must use it to prepare for the future. If this is lived out to its logical conclusion, we avoid enjoyment not only now but forever.

Avoid the temptation of wishing, hoping, and regretting—the most common tactics for evading the present. Abstain from the ritual of idealizing the future, which leads only to disappointment.

Invest in the present. The right time is any time. The best time is now. It is not necessary to surrender tomorrow or next year, but abandon yourself to God's presence and His will as it unfolds in your life moment to moment.

❀ ――――――――――――――――――――――――

*This moment is precious, Lord. You have given it to me and, along with myself, I give it back to You.*

❧

*I have learned to be satisfied with what I have.*
*Philippians 4:11b (TEV)*

W̲hy are there so few truly content people? One reason may be that many of us spend
too much time practicing being unhappy. Also,
we do not accept the real meaning of leisure
and give ourselves permission to enjoy life. We
don't spend enough time and energy practicing
being happy.

The apostle Paul said, "I have learned to be
content, whatever the circumstances may be."
For years I read that section of Scripture in
wonder and awe of this saint who had this gift
of being able to be content amid difficulties. I
didn't realize that this was not a natural, easy gift
for Paul. It was a trait he developed through
diligence and practice. He realized that, like
every good thing, contentment takes practice
and determination.

❧ _____

*I have a long way to go before I can say I am*
*satisfied no matter the circumstance. Teach me*
*godly contentment.*

✲

*I run in the path of your commands, for you have set my heart free. Psalm 119:32*

Research, I understand, has "proven scientifically" that it is impossible for the bumblebee to fly. Based on body size, density, shape, weight, wingspan, and speed of the wings, it is aeronautically impossible for this creature to get off the ground. However, someone forgot to notify the bumblebee.

When I read this I thought of the many times I've grounded myself by simply not appropriating some of the promises given to me. As Paul said, "We are sons of freedom. Christ has set us free, and we are called to stay free." We, too, were made for flying.

What we need is enough self-forgetfulness, enough abandonment, enough audacity to do the same. We need more Christian bumblebees.

✲ ──────────────────────────

*Get me off the ground, Lord. Help me fly.*

❈

*There is a time for everything, and a season for
every activity under heaven. Ecclesiastes 3:1*

I once read a thought-provoking article
entitled, "If You Are 35, You Have 500 Days to
Live." Its thesis was that when you subtract the
time spent sleeping working, tending to personal matters, hygiene, odd chores, medical matters,
eating, traveling, and miscellaneous time-stealers,
in the next thirty-six years you will have rough-
ly the equivalent of only five hundred days left
to spend as you wish.

All of us are given exactly the same amount
of time each day—24 hours, or 1,440 minutes,
or 86,400 seconds. No matter how each of us
deals with it. Each of us has both different purposes and different capacities for time, but in
God's eyes, none of us are more important than
another. He made each of us special, one-of-a-
kind human beings.

❈ ────────────────────────────

*Thank You for the gift of time. Teach me
how to use it for Your glory.*

❧

*For you were once darkness, but now you are light in the Lord. Live as children of light.*
**Ephesians 5:8**

How many times have we allowed our lives to settle into "Almost Christianity"? Because of the difficulty of the task, because of fear of accountability to others, because of defensiveness and unwillingness to live up to the demands of Scripture and of God Himself, slowly and imperceptibly we become very good at excusing ourselves. We pray almost believing and walk through our days as if He were almost risen.

The great problem with Jesus' message is not that it cannot be understood, but that it can. The difficulty is not one of which translation we read, but whether or not we translate what we know into life-style.

❧ _____

*Help me translate Your message into the very core of my life today, Jesus.*

❈

*Trust in the Lord with all your heart and lean
not on your own understanding; in all your
ways acknowledge him, and he will make
your paths straight. Proverbs 3:5, 6*

One night I was speaking about the genuine, concrete, tangible, unextinguishable joy I've discovered in the process of my life journey and a man came up to me afterwards and said, "You almost make me want to fall into a crevasse so I can discover how special life really is."

I don't recommend this particular process. Each of us gets a second chance every day, if we would just open our eyes to the possibilities. Each of us is his or her own story. Allow God to write His unique and indelible story in your life.

❈ ——————————————————————

*Write Your story on my life with indelible ink,
God of my past, present, and future.*

*The Lord will guide you always; he will satisfy your needs in a sun-scorched land and will strengthen your frame. You will be like a well-watered garden, like a spring whose waters never fail. Isaiah 58:11*

In the 1952 Olympics a young Hungarian boy looked down his pistol barrel and split the bull's-eye again and again; he just couldn't miss. With that perfect right hand and eye coordination, he won a gold medal. Six months later he lost his right arm. But in Melbourne four years later he came back and split the bull's-eye again and again, winning his second gold medal with his left hand. He chose not to be limited by his limitations.

Necessity is the author of change. Sometimes we only learn because we have to. Our level of joy (and therefore strength and healing) is directly proportionate to our level of acceptance. Our attitude is the key.

---

*Forgive me for letting my limitations—real or imagined—limit my commitment to You.*

☙❧

*Finally, be strong in the Lord and in his*
*mighty power. Ephesians 6:10*

In rock climbing there is a technical term called a "commitment move." Often it's the crux move of the climb. Handholds seem scarce and footholds appear nonexistent. The tendency is to "bogart"—to freeze, to panic, to wait until exhaustion causes you, the climber, to quit the climb. You have a rope around you that will keep you from ever falling more than a few inches. But still, your first feeling is to bogart. On our Summit Expedition courses, the staff will constantly encourage the climber to "go for it." "Don't bogart! Give it your best shot!" And on a commitment move, you've either got to go for it or come off the climb.

What's your commitment move these days?

☙❧ ─────────────────────────────

*Lord, because I can make my move, confident of*
*Your power, I'm going to "go for it!"*

❀

*But my trust is in you, O Lord; you are
my God. I am always in your care.
Psalm 31:14, 15a (TEV)*

Jeanette Harvey has spent her life in a
wheelchair. She says that many people look at
the limitations of being disabled, rather than the
assets. She is now a very successful career
woman, but it has not been achieved without a
fight, without pain, or without suffering from
the double distinction of being disabled and
female.

Among the "assets that result from disability"
Jeanette names the limitation of choice, which
makes it easier to focus all one's energy on the
possible instead of diluting and scattering it.
Both a light bulb and a laser beam are essential-
ly light energy, but while we hold our hands in
front of a light bulb without danger of being
burned, there are laser beams that can burn
through eighteen inches of solid steel. The difference is a matter of focus.

❀ _____

*Focus me, Lord, that Your light in
me will not be diffused.*

❁

*For when I was hungry, you gave me food; when
thirsty, you gave me drink; when I was a stranger
you took me into your home, when naked you
clothed me; when I was ill you came to my
help, when in prison you visited me.*
*Matthew 25:35, 36 (NEB)*

We live in a society that looks only on
the surfaces. But pain, if allowed, produces an
identification with the suffering of others, and
even with Christ, that we could not experience
in any other way. One is allowed to see dignity
in the midst of human struggle and see beyond
the false barriers that are oftentimes imposed
between human beings. If our maturity grows,
perhaps we even learn to see Christ in each
other and even in ourselves.

In the inevitable ache of the world, I never
cease to be amazed by the use of first person
singular in Matthew 25.

❁ ───────────────────────────

*What a wonder, Jesus, that in serving a suffering
world we are serving You!*

*Dear brothers, is your life full of difficulties and temptations? Then be happy, for when the way is rough, your patience has a chance to grow.*
*James 1:2, 3 (TLB)*

In 1962 research scientists Victor and Mildred Goertzel studied 413 famous and exceptionally gifted people to learn what produced such lives. The patterns which emerged from the study were startling. For example, approximately eighty percent of the later-famous children loathed school. Seven out of ten came from homes riddled with traumas such as missing or argumentative parents, poverty, and physical handicaps. Virtually all of them had overcome severe difficulties in order to become the people they were called to be.

Perhaps God gives us difficulties in order to give us the opportunity to know who we really are and who we really can be.

---

*Then I will thank You for the difficulties of my life and ask You to use them in my personal growth.*

***The word of the Lord came to me, saying, "Before I formed you in the womb I knew you, before you were born I set you apart; I appointed you as a prophet to the nations." "Ah, Sovereign Lord," I said, "I do not know how to speak; I am only a child." Jeremiah 1:4–6***

The heroes of the Bible were not knights in shining armor nor persons born with golden tongues nor giants lumpy with great muscles. They were ordinary people with goose bump courage who were invaded by the living God. When their circumstances seemed to overwhelm them, they rose to the occasion and gave the glory to God.

Amidst all the difficulties of modern day living, the story continues today. The great ones today are ordinary folk who have opened their lives up to God's presence and who do not simply tolerate difficulties, but lean into them.

*Sovereign Lord, I want to be one of those ordinary people who lean into difficulties, whose lives are open to be invaded by You.*

❧

*Therefore we do not lose heart. Though outwardly we are wasting away, yet inwardly we are being renewed day by day. II Corinthians 4:16*

Life is difficult. There is no way to get around it. We need to remind ourselves of it each day. Hence, it requires that we have something or Someone within us to encounter the mishaps and transcend them.

I simply believe that there is a mystery of the ordinary, that the commonplace is full of wonder, and that this life we call Christian is different from what we think it is. It is infinitely more subtle, more powerful, more dangerous, more magnificent, more exciting, more humorous, more delicious, more adventurous, more involved, and more troublesome than most of us think. To live fully this life that God has given us, no matter what circumstances may be, can be a rare and ennobling experience.

❧ ————————————————————

*I will not lose heart, Lord. I will count on You to encounter and transcend the difficulties.*

✿

*I can do everything through him who gives
me strength. Philippians 4:13*

It's only by cracking our very nature that
God is able to even begin to make us vessels for
His living word. We are called to be crucified
with Christ.

When I was younger and struggling hard
with that concept, I asked a saintly, elderly
woman, "Why, if my old nature has been crucified with Christ, does it continue to keep on
wiggling?"

She smiled and said in a quiet voice, "You
must remember, Tim, that crucifixion is a slow
death."

A. W. Tozer says there are three marks of one
who is crucified. One, he is facing in only one
direction. Two, he can never turn back. And
three, he no longer has any plans of his own.

✿ _____

*Lord, I find myself resisting my crucifixion. Yet, I
know that in You is the strength to go to the cross.*

*Give thanks to the Lord, for he is good;*
*his love endures forever. Psalm 107:1*

Sometimes we seem to treat our faith as if it were an artificial limb that we strap on each day. Though it helps us stumble along, it never really becomes a part of us. Whatever happened to that holy wonder, that appetite for the sacred? Have we grown blind to the sacredness of everyday things and of everyday people? Where is our appetite for stillness which, as T. S. Eliot says, "is the turning point, is where the dance is." What are we waiting for?

I've known people whose lives are full of hardship and yet they made it sound beautiful. Their courage is evidenced in little commitments they make every day, little acts of gratitude and wonder—in spite of their circumstances. They make life come alive for those around them.

---

*When I take time to look, I am awed by what I see of You in the ordinariness of my day.*

❈

*We are asking God that you may see things, as it were, from his point of view by being given spiritual insight and understanding. We also pray that your outward lives, which men see, may bring credit to your master's name, and that you may bring joy to his heart by bearing genuine Christian fruit, and that your knowledge of God may grow yet deeper.*
*Colossians 1:9b, 10 (Phillips)*

How often we limit ourselves before we even start.

A seventy-year-old woman in northern California who just started running marathons, was eagerly looking forward to the adventure that lay ahead of her. Bruce Jennings cycled from the west coast of the United States to the east coast. What made it unusual was that he had only one leg. Pete Strudwick runs marathons in some of his spare time. Pete was born without hands or feet.

Many of us are more handicapped by our attitudes than by any physical inconvenience.

❈ ————————————————————

*Forgive me, God, for letting such small matters handicap my life.*

❧❧

*So Moses thought, "I will go over and see this
strange sight—why the bush does not burn up."
When the Lord saw that he had gone over to
look, God called to him from within the bush,
"Moses, Moses!" Exodus 3:3, 4*

We tragically have thought that becoming
a Christian is a matter of conforming to a certain pattern of behavior, a certain image of preconceived holiness. Our problem is that we've
continually viewed the incredible power of God
from a distance. God called Moses by name—
but when did He call him? That is the key. Did
He call Moses while Moses stood admiring at a
distance? No, God didn't reveal Himself until
Moses "turned aside to see."

❧❧ ———————————————————————

*Help me to notice the "burning bushes," God.
I want to experience Your power up close.*

❀

*But you have an anointing from the Holy One,*
*and all of you know the truth. I John 2:20*

No truths are simple, especially those of
Scripture. But as we pursue them and participate in them more fully, they begin to reveal to
us a life deeper and more integrated than we
ever could have known otherwise.

The Bible says if we know the truth it will
set us free. There is something qualitatively different between knowing and just believing.
Knowing in both the Old and New Testaments
implies intimacy, deep understanding, and experience. It implies an element of participation
beyond mere cerebral assent. It is belief which
has matured and taken root, and has been translated from mere cognition to a new kind of
power.

❀ ────────────────────────────────

*Oh Holy One, let me know You in a way*
*I have yet to experience.*

# THE
# IMPORTANCE
# OF
# PROBLEMS

❧

*Because the patriarchies were jealous of Joseph,
they sold him as a slave into Egypt. But God
was with him and rescued him from all his troubles. He gave Joseph wisdom and enabled him to
gain the goodwill of Pharaoh king of Egypt; so
he made him ruler over Egypt and all his palace.
Acts 7:9, 10*

We cannot afford to sit back and let
problems "solve themselves." We serve a living
God who enables us to do all things through
Christ who lives within us. The Bible is basically
a book about problems—lots of problems—and
how God enabled men and women to solve
them. The basic "attitude" of Scripture is that
our problems are normal and vital and that God
can help us solve them. Our current problems
are not a surprise to God. They may break His
heart, as they sometimes break ours, but they
don't surprise Him. As someone has said, "God
never has to say 'Oops!'"

❧ ─────────────────────────────

*You are not surprised by the problems of my life,
Lord, and You hold the solutions in Your hand.*

*Dear friends, do not be surprised at the painful trial you are suffering, as though something strange were happening to you. I Peter 4:12*

The Bible clearly teaches that to have faith is to have problems. This contradicts those who today preach a "health-and-wealth gospel" implying that the more faith we have the less problems we will have. Actually the opposite may be true. Daniel's faith may have gotten him out of the lion's den, but don't forget his faith got him into the lion's den as well. From the first book until the last, the Bible is filled with examples of how God helped people solve problems.

Yes, we live with constant problems, some of them because we serve the Lord, but through them we gain repeated opportunities to show the power of Jesus Christ in our lives.

*I pray that You will demonstrate Your power through my problems, Jesus.*

❈

*When you pass through the waters, I will be with you; and when you pass through the rivers, they will not sweep over you. When you walk through the fire, you will not be burned; the flames will not set you ablaze. Isaiah 43:2*

The Bible assumes that we are going to have problems. Isaiah didn't say, "If you go through problems." He said, "When you go through problems, God will be there with you." The Bible tells by example after example that God allows us to encounter numerous problems—big, small, medium, long-term, short-term, or whatever—in order to help us discover a new fullness of life in Him. Problems are a very practical and direct way to experience God's power in our lives.

❈ ——————————————————————

*Lord, I cling to Your promise that You will be with me through my problems.*

# The Importance of Problems

*Who, then, is the man that fears the Lord? He will instruct him in the way chosen for him.*
**Psalm 25:12**

Most people think of problems as something bad, as some terrible interruption in their lives which they wish they did not have to endure. In truth, problems in and of themselves are not necessarily bad. It is interesting to note the actual Greek root of the word *problem*, namely, *probalein*, means "to throw, to drive, or to thrust forward." Problems are the very means by which God changes us, transforms us, and drives us forward. Without problems, there would be no growth.

Thomas Merton, one of the great spiritual writers of our century, said: "A life without problems is hopeless." It is vital to realize that problems are not only inevitable but also important for us. They play a far more significant role in our lives, in our growth, than we would ever imagine.

*Thank You that You can use my problems to help me grow in faith, Dear Father.*

❁

*Therefore it is necessary to choose one of the men
who have been with us the whole time the Lord
Jesus went in and out among us. . . . So they
proposed two men: Joseph called Barsabbas
(also known as Justus) and Matthias. Then they
prayed. . . . Then they cast lots, and the lot fell to
Matthias; so he was added to the eleven apostles.*
*Acts 1:21, 23, 24a, 26*

I believe that the greatest thing that God
has given us, outside of His Son, is each other. If
you want to improve your problem-solving
techniques, your parenting, your work, or any
other area of your life, get together with someone else and pray about and brainstorm the
possibilities.

Together you can carry any idea a little further—make it a little better. You can look for
ways to combine two or more ideas to make an
even better idea.

Most of the best ideas in the world haven't
happened yet.

❁ _____

*Lord, I am grateful for the people you've put in
my life to help me work through problems.*

*The eye is the lamp of the body. If your eyes are good, your whole body will be full of light. But if your eyes are bad, your whole body will be full of darkness. Matthew 6:22, 23a*

Are you filling your life "full of darkness" because your vision is too shortsighted? Are you only allowing yourself a limited view of your present circumstances and of yourself? Perhaps you are in danger of becoming the powerless victim of your problems. There is a life-changing solution that promises unimaginable power and freedom. Jesus says in Matthew 6:31-32, "So do not worry. . . . But seek first his kingdom and his righteousness, and all these things will be given to you as well."

We are asked to see beyond our own limited resources and opinions and to see our circumstances with the eyes of God. Once I recognize God's providence, He can transfigure my impossibilities into attainable goals.

---

*Show me my situation through spiritual glasses, God, that my impossibilities can become possibilities.*

❧

*A simple man believes anything, but a prudent man gives thought to his steps. Proverbs 14:15*

In our everyday life we make constant assumptions. When we come to certain problems we say "it's not logical," "it's not practical," "that's not my area," "I'm not creative," or "we've never done it that way before." Often we assume that "speaking is more important than listening," that "being busy is more important than being still," that "big is better than small," that "new is better than old," that "some place far away is better than right here," or that "fast is better than slow."

Christians can sometimes be very susceptible to assumptions. Because we look to God for guidance, we sometimes assume that there is "one" way to do things, that for certain situations there is one "right" answer.

What assumptions are you making that hamper your ability to solve problems creatively?

❧ ──────────────────────────

*Lord, where are my assumptions hampering Your work in my life?*

***Glorify the Lord with me; let us exalt his name together. Psalm 34:3***

Sometimes we magnify our problems instead of our Lord. We humans have the capacity to distort almost anything. Consider the following paraphrased portion of a well-known verse in Psalm 34 (the Hansel version): "Oh come let us magnify our problems together. Let us talk about them until they become impossible." We magnify our problems by doubt, anxiety, worry, procrastination, and self-preoccupation. How many times have you heard someone insinuate, "My problems are worse than anyone else's."

Our problems take on their proper proportion when we share them, as accurately as possible, with someone else.

---

*Lord, often my problems look so much bigger than they are. Remind me that You see them in the right perspective.*

❧

*I plead with Euodia and I plead with Syntyche to agree with each other in the Lord. Yes, and I ask you, loyal yokefellow, help these women who have contended at my side in the cause of the gospel. Philippians 4:2, 3a*

It is much nicer to be in love than in an automobile accident, a tight girdle, a higher tax bracket, or a holding pattern over Atlanta. But not if the object of your love doesn't love you back.

Because we are human beings, there is no such thing as an isolated, single, untangled relational problem. Because we are all so different, conflict is inevitable.

Relationships are the essence of the quality of our lives. Whether we are single, married, divorced, widowed, or somewhere in between, our relationships form the backbone that gives meaning to our lives. And the problems with them are not solved once for all, but piece by piece.

❧ ───────────────

*Father God, I thank You for the people You have brought into my life—for the relationships that inspire, challenge, and sustain me.*

# THE IMPORTANCE OF PROBLEMS

◆◆◆

*In your anger do not sin: Do not let the sun go down while you are still angry. Ephesians 4:26*

In relational problems there is no such thing as an "appropriate" time. The Bible says not to let the sun go down on your anger. We must recognize when we have a problem and find the first available moment to discuss it while it's still in its proper proportion. Leftover problems, like leftover meatloaf, not only grow stale but also begin to mold.

*Love* is a four-letter word spelled *t-i-m-e*. To avoid moldy relational problems, we need to spend time in listening deeply to each other.

◆◆◆ ――――――――――――――――――――――――――

*Help me to face those unresolved problems with certain persons, Lord. Give me the courage to go to them and the grace to listen, to ask forgiveness, and to forgive.*

***And now, dear lady, I am not writing you a new command but one we have had from the beginning. I ask that we love one another.***
***II John 5***

When we put God, who is love, in the center of our relationships He transforms them. He empowers us to influence each other's lives.

God's love makes us fearless, and where there is no fear there is true understanding. This love will never be contained nor understood. It is available to all and can literally produce miracles in relationships. Love casts out fear. It covers a multitude of sins. Love is absolutely invincible. "There is no difficulty that enough love will not conquer, no disease that enough love cannot heal, no door that enough love will not open, no gulf that enough love will not bridge, no wall that enough love will not throw down, no sin that enough love will not redeem."

---

*Empower me, through Your love, to bridge the gulf of misunderstanding between me and certain others in my life.*

*Bear with each other and forgive whatever griev-ances you may have against one another. Forgive as the Lord forgave you. Colossians 3:13*

We can respond to conflict in two ways. Jordan and Margaret Paul point out in their book, *Do I Have to Give up Me to Be Loved by You?* that when faced with a conflict we will either try to protect or learn. Conflict does not cause problems in relationships, instead problems evolve from how we respond to the conflict. "Seeing conflict as opportunity rather than as a calamity puts it in a new light."

Our relational problem solving will always be unsuccessful as long as our primary interest is protective. We must commit ourselves to open-ness and learning.

When we assume responsibility for our prob-lems we can explore relational difficulties as process rather than only seek an "answer."

*Lord, help me see conflict as a way to learn, and give me a spirit of forgiveness.*

❧

*Submit to one another out of reverence*
*for Christ. Ephesians 5:21*

A friend of mine and his wife were going through great difficulties which eventually led to a divorce. I was spending much time with David trying to listen and learn and be of some help to him. My wife shocked me by saying, "David will never begin to solve some of his problems with Katherine until he realizes that it is 100 percent his fault."

I quickly came to his defense saying, "I know David has made some big mistakes, but she's got to have some of the responsibility too."

My wife responded, "Yes, Katherine is also 100-percent responsible for the relationship."

She was right. God's solution is for each of us to be totally responsible for the relationship because the only person you can ever change is yourself.

---

*It's easy to see what responsibility others should take in my relationships with them, Father. I need Your help to be responsible for my 100 percent.*

***Admit your faults to one another and pray for each other so that you may be healed.***
***James 5:16a (TLB)***

Carl Jung said, "The only person I cannot help is one who blames others." That simple statement knocked my socks off! It has about it a profound simplicity. When we blame others, we make it difficult, if not impossible, to solve our problems.

When problems inevitably invade our lives, we must resist the temptation to accuse others or blame ourselves . . . or God.

We need to focus on the problem, not the person. If there have been failures, we need to confess them in ourselves and forgive them in others. Then we put the problem in perspective and can get on with problem solving.

*Lord, how often I resort to blaming—others or even myself—when You are waiting for me to bring the problem to You.*

***

*Restore to me the joy of your salvation and grant me a willing spirit, to sustain me. Psalm 51:12*

I overheard a golfer saying, "What an incredible course this is. It has a wicked dog leg, two huge sand traps, and a pond." He went on describing all the obstacles of the course, and then he said, "I love it! It's the most exciting course I've ever played!" The course was difficult and it brought out his best golfing skills. With the right attitude about the course, he turned something difficult into something fun and stimulating.

Life is a process: a complex, ever-continuing, ever-changing set of problems. The choice is not *if* you'll accept problems, but *how*! Your attitude determines whether or not you will succeed. William James said, "Perhaps the greatest discovery of this century is that if you can change your attitude, you can change your life."

***

*When it comes to my problems, I need an attitude adjustment, Lord.*

*For by the grace given me I say to every one of you: Do not think of yourself more highly than you ought, but rather think of yourself with sober judgment, in accordance with the measure of faith God has given you. Romans 12:3*

One of the most liberating discoveries of my life was that problems can be potential blessings. They can be a means for growth. I also know that in Christ I have the capacity to be a very capable problem solver.

The Bible encourages us to have a sane estimate of our abilities. Many people interpret this to mean that we should think less of ourselves. In having a sane estimate of our abilities, we realize the amazing things that God can do in us and through us. When we do that, we become much less intimidated by problems because we know that God is not only for us but in us. Therefore, I am not afraid to fail.

*Oh God, when I remember that You actually live in me, my limitations become Your opportunities.*

✦

*Oh, the depth of the riches of the wisdom and knowledge of God! How unsearchable his judgments, and his paths beyond tracing out! "Who has known the mind of the Lord? Or who has been his counselor?" . . . For from him and through him and to him are all things. To him be the glory forever! Amen. Romans 11:33, 34, 36*

We think that if we commit our lives to God, He will work things out for us so that everything will run smoothly for us without problems. When it doesn't work that way we ask, "why?" We find it easy to believe that unbelievers or scoundrels have problems but inevitably we ask why does a just and loving God permit us to experience hard times. We are always ready to praise Him for our blessings, but we fail to see that so often our problems are really blessings in disguise. For without problems there would be no learning, no growth, no opportunity to change.

✦ ───────────────────────────

*I give you glory, wise and loving God—You take problems and turn them into blessings!*

*[Job's] wife said to him, "Are you still holding on to your integrity? Curse God and die!" He replied, "You are talking like a foolish woman. Shall we accept good from God, and not trouble?" Job 2:9, 10a*

I asked a good friend what he thought life would be like without problems. He said, "I think a person with no problems would be in serious trouble. If you think about it, it's our problems that provide us with growth opportunities. Relationships within a family without problems would lack depth and the children could not possibly mature into adults without the opportunity to solve many problems."

Perhaps like me, you have a tendency to want to protect your children from having problems. Yet on a deeper level we must hope that they encounter significant problems in their lives, so that they can become mature people of God.

---

*Lord, I do want to protect those I love from having to deal with problems. Help me to release my loved ones and their problems to You.*

❀

*Show me your ways, O Lord, teach me your
paths; guide me in your truth and teach me,
for you are God my Savior, and my hope is
in you all day long. Psalm 25:4, 5*

Change will be the norm in the ever
increasingly complex future that faces all of us.
We will no longer be able to solve today's and
tomorrow's problems with yesterday's solutions.
Nevertheless, we have a choice. We can either
spend our time and energy complaining about
how things aren't as easy as they used to be or
we can begin to employ and develop some of
our God-given creative abilities and thus discover new ideas, new answers, and new solutions.
As someone once said, "If you do what you've
always done and think what you've always
thought, there's a good chance you'll get what
you've always got."

❀ ─────────────────────────

*Open my heart and mind to new ways of
looking at my difficulties, Father.*

❊

*But they that wait upon the Lord shall renew
their strength; they shall mount up with wings
as eagles; they shall run, and not be weary;
and they shall walk, and not faint.*
*Isaiah 40:31 (KJV)*

On a Summit Expedition wilderness pro-
gram for the physically handicapped, I was in
excruciating pain, beginning to think, "Why
me?" when I looked over and saw Pam Dahl
ready to take on her first rock-climbing challenge.

Because of cerebral palsy Pam has never
walked, and could not use her arms in climbing.

Our instructors tied her onto the rope at the
bottom of the cliff and then for the next hour
and a half she inched her way up the rock. At the
top, instructors helped her over to a rock where
she curled her bent legs underneath her and said,
"That was fun. Let's do it again."

Needless to say, I became rather embarrassed
about my "pity party."

Changing our perspective sets us free to see
problems as they really are.

❊ ────────────────────────────

*Lord, set me free from my whining to see
my life from Your perspective.*

*You will keep in perfect peace him whose mind is steadfast, because he trusts in you. Isaiah 26:3*

Y̶ou are "hooked" when your emotions dominate and you're more concerned about your feelings than you are about the problem involving the feelings.

When you are emotionally hooked, you imprison yourself within a very narrow view of the problem. When you find yourself emotionally hooked, first focus on God and His perspective on the problem and then try to find out what the problem really is. Go for a walk, get some exercise, back away from the problem until you can see it from a more detached point of view. I've found that it helps to focus on a favorite Bible passage such as the one above.

*"Unhook me," Lord, as I focus my mind on You and not on my problems.*

*A simple man believes anything, but a prudent man gives thought to his steps. Proverbs 14:15*

When you face problems, there is equal danger in underdefining them as there is in overdefining them.

Simple answers are not necessarily simplistic answers. Band-Aids are a simple, effective solution for cuts and scrapes, but they don't do a thing for cancer. Likewise simplistic answers don't address the real issues of a problem. If you use them, you will probably cover up what you don't understand rather than take the time to see the problem clearly. Therefore, you won't know enough about the problem to be able to sort the necessary from the unnecessary.

To simplify a problem means simply to remove that which clutters up your thinking.

*Unclutter my thinking, Lord, and help me see my problem for what it is.*

❦

*So, humble yourselves under God's strong hand,
and in his own good time he will lift you up.
You can throw the whole weight of your anxieties
upon him for you are his personal concern.
I Peter 5:6, 7 (Phillips)*

*If the only tool you have is a hammer, you
tend to see every problem as a nail.*
ABRAHAM MASLOW

Someone once said that the mind is like a
parachute; it works best when it's open.
Opening windows within yourself opens countless possibilities as you consider your problems.
Many people suffer from what could rightly be
called "a hardening of the categories." They
aren't capable of seeing—or they refuse to see—
the whole picture. Little do they realize that
these self-imposed limitations greatly restrict
their problem-solving abilities.

Keeping a broad perspective will definitely
influence how you will approach a problem—
and indeed, its final outcome.

❦ ─────────────────────────────

*Open my mind to the possibilities when I see Your
strong hand holding me and my problems, God.*

*Now I want you to know, brothers, that what has happened to me has really served to advance the gospel. Philippians 1:12*

Paul makes a radical statement here, implying that our suffering is actually a privilege because it brings us into a deeper relationship with Jesus Christ. Then he says, "I keep going on, trying to grasp that purpose for which Christ Jesus grasped me. . . . I forget all that lies behind me and with hands outstretched to whatever lies ahead I go straight for the goal—my reward, the honor of my high calling by God and Christ Jesus."

That is perspective! Paul considered his problems an advantage, and he realized that whatever happened had to be left behind. He reached forward eagerly to whatever the future held so that he could maintain his focus, that of deepening his relationship with Christ.

---

*I want to know You better, Jesus, and I want to have more of Paul's perspective as I look at the difficulties of my life.*

❀

*Whatever happens, dear friends, be glad in the Lord. I never get tired of telling you this and it is good for you to hear it again and again.*
*Philippians 3:1 (TLB)*

I'm always amazed at Paul's perspective on life. The book of Philippians was written after Paul had been shipwrecked, stoned, and beaten. It was written from a prison where Paul was chained to a Roman guard, and yet, in Philippians he uses the words "joy" and "rejoice" more than nineteen times. He couldn't have done this without seeing his problems from God's perspective.

Is there a problem you're wrestling with now in which your perspective is limited? Is there another way to look at the problem? Can you reframe it? Can you look at it from a larger perspective? In fact, can you see that problem from God's perspective? Being able to see our problems from God's perspective can change the situation entirely.

❀ ───────────────────────────

*My problems look smaller when I am rejoicing in You.*

# The Importance of Problems

❧

*But when you pray, you must believe and not doubt at all. Whoever doubts is like a wave in the sea that is driven and blown about by the wind. James 1:6, 7 (TEV)*

I received a letter from a relatively new friend. In it she said, "No, unfortunately my problems didn't all disappear, but some changes have happened. As a successful professional woman who has been single for twelve years, I was reminded (as I have been for years) that I try too hard to control and make things happen my way. I again turned it all over to the Lord, but this time with perhaps a little more trust— and some remarkable things began to happen."

Like my friend, I constantly need to be reminded to let go, to turn things over to Him, and to see my problems from His perspective.

❧ ———————————————————————

*Help me, Lord, to let go of my problems and really trust them to You.*

❖

*Commit your way to the Lord; trust in him*
*and he will do this. Psalm 37:5a*

We live in the midst of alarms; anxiety
clouds the future; we expect some new disaster
with each newspaper we read." That statement
sounds current, but it was reported in a newspaper
per more than a hundred years ago. Its author?
Abraham Lincoln.

When anxiety about problems clouds our
future we need to ask ourselves these three
questions:

1. What is our attitude toward the problem?
2. Who is in control of the problem? Who is
   really responsible for it?
3. Where is the Lord in relationship to the
   problem?

We must be better problem solvers than those
before us. We must remember that God isn't
wringing His hands wondering what to do
next.

❖ _____

*Lord, it's so easy to forget that I can commit my*
*problems to You—that You are in the*
*problem-solving business.*

❧

*So David triumphed over the*
*Philistine with a sling and a stone.*
*I Samuel 17:50a*

The flood waters rose, but Mr. Brown sat on his porch. A man in a rowboat said, "Jump in! I'll take you to safety."

"I'm fine, thank you," said Mr. Brown. "God will take care of me."

The waters rose higher as a Coast Guard boat came by. "Mr. Brown, we'll take you to safety."

Mr. Brown smiled, "Thanks, but God will take care of me."

The waters rose and Mr. Brown had to sit on his roof. A helicopter pilot shouted, "Climb up this ladder and we'll save you."

Mr. Brown smiled, and said, "Thanks, but God will take care of me."

Mr. Brown drowned. In heaven Mr. Brown asked God, "Why didn't You save me?"

And God said, "I sent you a rowboat, a Coast Guard boat, and a helicopter!"

❧ _____

*Forgive me God, for ignoring the resources*
*You are providing me to solve my problems.*

❧

*I will praise the Lord, who counsels me.*
*Psalm 16:7a*

Attitude is everything. I phoned a special
friend of mine who is a developer during what
was probably the most difficult time of his life.
"How're you doing, Jack?" His response surprised me. "Terrific! In fact, unbelievable!" I was
so caught off guard by his response that I hardly
knew what to say. "Jack, has the market gone
up?" (It was my understanding that this was the
toughest time possible in his business.) "Has
there been a significant change in your situation?" "No," Jack said. "It's just that I realized
what a phenomenal opportunity I have to learn.
I probably have the privilege of learning more
right now because of all these opportunities dis-
guised as problems than at any other time in my
life. It's really a privilege isn't it, Tim?"

❧ _____

*I praise You, Father, for the opportunities You are*
*providing me right now to learn.*

# The Importance of Problems

*With great power the apostles continued to testify to the resurrection of the Lord Jesus, and much grace was upon them all. There were no needy persons among them. For from time to time those who owned lands or houses sold them, brought the money from the sales and put it at the apostles' feet, and it was distributed to anyone as he had need. Acts 4:33–35*

Life is a never-ending, always changing series of continual problems, but we can apply a deliberate and systematic approach to solving problems that still leaves plenty of room for spontaneity and flexibility.

Problems can become the "fuel" for the future. We learn from them.

Since problems are the core of our existence, problem solving is too.

Ultimately, we can take what we've learned and share God's immense love for the world by getting involved in some of the needs around us.

---

*Thank You for being a practical God—that You are interested in using me to help meet the basic need of the world.*

❧

***The spiritual man makes judgments about all
things, but he himself is not subject to any
man's judgment: "For who has known the
mind of the Lord that he may instruct him?"
I Corinthians 2:15, 16a***

The most critical step in problem solving is
to learn how to meet problems head on. Lean
into them, face them squarely, and attack them
creatively. Your choice of attitude is the single
most important ingredient affecting your abilities as a problem solver, and you are the only
one who has that choice. Your attitude must be
one of boldness.

The Bible says that we can have the mind of
Christ. Jesus never ran away from anything, anybody, or any problem. God doesn't ask us if we
will accept the inevitable problems of life. They
are a reality. The only question we have to
address is how we confront our problems.

❧ ──────────────────────────────

*Jesus, as You faced life head-on, never flinching, help
me to boldly face my problems in Your strength.*

*Test me, O Lord, and try me, examine my heart and my mind; for your love is ever before me, and I walk continually in your truth. Psalm 26:2, 3*

Whether your problems are as simple as a shoe coming apart or as complicated as a life coming apart, you have problems.

Lloyd Ogilvie says that we all have, to a greater or lesser degree, a profound misunderstanding of the positive purpose of problems. "Until we grapple with this gigantic problem, we will be helpless victims of our problems all through our lives."

Perhaps this is why the writer of the Book of James says in essence, "Consider yourself blessed when you have lots of problems—for you know that these will serve to develop your faith, your endurance, and your steadfastness. In fact, if you hang in there with those problems, you will become competent and fully developed—lacking in nothing."

*As I walk in Your truth, Father, I look to You to use my problems to develop my faith, my endurance, my steadfastness.*

❀

*. . . make the most of every opportunity.*
***Colossians 4:5b***

It all depends on how we look at our problems. A shoe salesman was sent to Africa into a territory previously unreached by this company. The eager salesman aggressively went about his work of trying to sell shoes. Three weeks later, however, he phoned the president and said, "Send me a plane ticket, I'm coming back. Didn't you realize that people over here don't wear shoes? This job is impossible."

The company sent him a return ticket but some months later hired a woman in his place. Three weeks later she phoned the company's president and said, "This place is amazing, the possibilities are endless. What an unbelievable opportunity! Do you realize that the people over here don't have shoes? This job is wonderful!"

❀ ─────────────────────────────

*Oh to see possibilities instead of problems
when I face difficult times, Lord!*

❈

*. . . he will watch over your life; the Lord will watch over your coming and going both now and forevermore. Psalm 121:7b, 8*

In the Chinese language, whole words are written with a symbol. Often two completely different symbols put together have a meaning quite different than either of their two separate components. For example, the symbols for *man* and for *woman* when combined mean *good*.

Likewise, when you take the symbol for *trouble* and *gathering crisis* and put them together they mean *opportunity*. As the answers to life always lie in the questions, so the opportunities of life lie in our problems.

❈ _____

*Lord, when I remember that You are in my life, I can see trouble turning into opportunity.*

*I cry aloud to the Lord; I lift up my voice to the Lord for mercy. I pour out my complaint before him; before him I tell my trouble. When my spirit grows faint within me, it is you who know my way. Psalm 142:1–3a*

Many large problems won't be solved in our lifetime, if they're solved at all. In spite of the extraordinary efforts of countless committed people, the solution to world hunger still eludes us.

When we encounter seemingly unsolvable problems in our lives, we need to turn to God and ask for His help with such questions as "How do I go on from here? How will I survive this pain and sorrow?" Often in the context of unsolvable problems we discover a new strength to our lives that is more profound than anything we've ever imagined or hoped for. In those moments we find a timeless coherence that is based on truths which do not come from us.

---

*Some of my problems are beyond me, Lord. I don't have answers. I look to You for strength to go on.*

❀

*Therefore, strengthen your feeble arms and weak knees. Make level paths for your feet.*
**Hebrews 12:12, 13a**

There are some very intelligent people who would rather live with problems than accept the challenge of solving them.

Actually, a problem is not a problem until you accept it as one. You must first realize that a problem exists and then be willing to do something about it. For example, in a seminary class recently I asked, "How many of you believe that world hunger is a problem?" Every hand went up. Then I asked, "How many of you are actually doing something about it?" Only a few hands went up. According to the problem-solving process, those who didn't raise their hands have not yet accepted hunger as a problem. To accept a problem means that you are willing to do something, that you are ready to actively involve yourself in the problem-solving process.

❀ ────────────────────────

*Help me to recognize those problems I haven't been willing to face, God. Strengthen my wimpy will.*

❀

*Pray also for me, that whenever I open my mouth, words may be given me so that I will fearlessly make known the mystery of the gospel, for which I am an ambassador in chains.*
*Ephesians 6:19, 20a*

Most of the greatest thoughts of the greatest thinkers of all time had to pass through the fire. Bunyan wrote *Pilgrim's Progress* from jail. Florence Nightingale, too ill to move from her bed, reorganized the hospitals of England. Semiparalyzed and under the constant menace of apoplexy, Pasteur was tireless in his attack on disease. American historian Francis Parkman's eyesight was so wretched that he could scrawl only a few gigantic words on a manuscript, yet he contrived to write twenty magnificent volumes of history. Sometimes it seems that when God is about to make preeminent use of a man or woman He puts them through the fire.

❀ ─────────────────────────────

*I have to admit, Lord, that I am not very willing to go through trouble in order to be useful to you. Work in my fearful heart.*

❁

*The righteous will flourish like a palm tree, they will grow like a cedar of Lebanon; planted in the house of the Lord, they will flourish in the courts of our God. Psalm 92:12, 13*

Certain religious circles today would have us believe that the ideal spiritual life is one where problems are instantaneously solved and miracles never cease.

Perhaps this has been true for some people. It has not been my experience. And according to my limited observations, it does not seem to be biblical. The Bible, above all else, seems to be a book of reality. And reality has the mark of difficulty.

On one side is the message of hope. "The righteous shall flourish like the palm tree"—but palm trees don't grow in beautiful forests, but in the desert. We are called to bear fruit—but we must recognize that the fruit tree grows in valleys, not on mountaintops.

❁ ───────────────────────

*May my desire be to experience all of what You have arranged for me that I might grow into a person whose life will shout Your glory!*

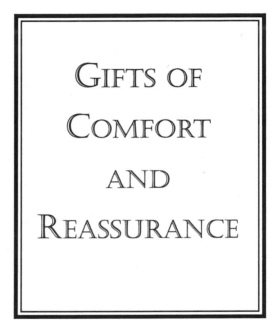

# GIFTS OF COMFORT AND REASSURANCE

❧

***Jesus Christ is the same yesterday and
today and forever. Hebrews 13:8***

Since Jesus is the same yesterday, today, and
tomorrow, I am quite convinced that since He
could calm the raging sea, He can also calm the
tumult raging within us that accompanies our
problems.

I need to relax, trust, let go. I need to look at
my problems from another angle, talk them over
with a friend. Talk them over with The Friend.
Remember: "Don't worry over anything whatever; whenever you pray tell God every detail of
your needs in thankful prayer, and the peace of
God, which surpasses human understanding,
will keep constant guard over your hearts and
minds as they rest in Christ Jesus" (Philippians
4:6, 7, Phillips)

❧ _____

*How often I let circumstances rob me of Your peace,
Jesus. Thank You for reminding me that it is
there for the trusting.*

❦

*Do not fret because of evil men or be envious
of those who do wrong. . . . Trust in the Lord
and do good; dwell in the land and enjoy safe
pasture. Delight yourself in the Lord and he will
give you the desires of your heart. Commit your
way to the Lord; trust in him and he will do
this. . . . Be still before the Lord and wait
patiently for him. Psalm 37:1, 3-5, 7a*

Here in this one passage in the Psalms are
five critical ingredients of "right attitude":

1. Do not fret and worry.
2. Trust in the Lord.
3. Take delight in Him.
4. Commit your way to the Lord.
5. Be still, rest in Him, and wait patiently.

The word *worry* actually means "to divide the
mind." We are told on countless occasions in
the Bible that if we pray and ask for God's wisdom, He will give it to us in abundance. So,
why do we worry?

Trust Him. Enjoy Him. Rest in Him.

❦ ————————————————————

*Why do I worry? Forgive my lack of trust.
Thank You for the gift of Your rest.*

❀

*I have loved you even as the Father has loved me.*
*Live within my love. John 15:9 (TLB)*

Near the end of his life, Robert Frost, the poet, was asked what was the most profound thought he'd ever had. Frost said, "Life goes on."

Karl Barth, a famous theologian and author of more than sixty volumes of theology, was asked a similar question. The young reporter who asked it realized that this was a somewhat ridiculous question to ask a man of such knowledge and renown. Nevertheless, the theologian, seeing this realization dawn on the reporter, said, "Yes, I do have a reply. I can respond to your question. The most profound thought I've ever had is, 'Jesus loves me, this I know, for the Bible tells me so.'"

❀ ───────────────────────────────

*Jesus, nothing in my life is more important*
*than the fact that You love me.*

✹

*Bring my sons from afar and my daughters from*
*the ends of the earth—everyone who is called by*
*my name, whom I created for my glory, whom I*
*formed and made. Isaiah 43:6b, 7*

We were designed for a relationship with the Father and, believe it or not, loneliness is one of the most powerful ways for us to fully understand and experience that. Sometimes the problem is that we are too full of ourselves— perhaps because we don't truly believe that God is enough, that His reality is sufficient on a daily, practical level. So we pursue our distractions and are on the way to becoming "functional atheists," no longer believing that God can fill our empty hearts. But all the while God waits for us to discover this simple fact: He made us for Himself!

✹ ———————————————————————

*I bear the mark of Your ownership, Lord. You made*
*me for Yourself and I am Yours.*

❧

*I cry to you, O Lord; I say, "You are my refuge,*
*my portion in the land of the living."*
**Psalm 142:5**

What would one conclude, I wonder, about a person who spent his whole life dissecting, analyzing, and advocating love, but who had never himself been in love? Is this the kind of Christian I am? Perhaps it describes all of us who never have time for solitude and prayer. We want people to do what only God can do. We want people to fill up that space within us that only God can fill.

Psalm 142 was written in a cave where David was hiding from King Saul. Alone, desperately lonely, frightened and ill at ease, he pours out his troubles to God. And God answers, not with earthly friends but simply with Himself.

❧ ───────────────────────────

*Lord, how often I have looked to the people in my*
*life to fill the space that only You can fill.*

❈

*Therefore encourage one another and build each
other up, just as in fact you are doing.
I Thessalonians 5:11*

I heard a pastor begin a sermon, "As it says
in Genesis, God said, 'Let there be light' and
there was light. And God said it was good. And
God said, 'Let the waters under the heavens be
gathered together into one place and let the dry
land appear.' And it was good. And finally, God
made man in His image. And he said, 'It is not
good.' "

The pastor paused, and I sat there somewhat
confused. "It is not good that the man should be
alone; I will make him a helper fit for him."

We were designed for relationships. We were
made to be with each other, to grow with each
other, to discover each other, to love each other,
and together we can work through life's
inevitable problems.

❈ _____

*Loving God, I thank You for the relationships that
enrich my life and encourage me to grow.*

❀

*May the God of hope fill you with all joy and peace as you trust in him, so that you may overflow with hope by the power of the Holy Spirit.*
**Romans 15:13**

When I learned to swim, I also had to learn how to float. My body was always capable of doing it, but I had to learn how to trust the water. Once I learned, it was easy, and the more I did it, the easier it got. My confidence grew with experience.

Living in Christ is like that. The more I do it—the more I really let go—the easier it gets. My confidence grows with experience. I can catch my breath, let go. Just as the water held me up to float, He who surrounds me does the work. I can just rest. I know that He will hold me because I have tested Him.

❀ ─────────────────────────────

*You are reminding me once again that, as I trust You, You are there to hold me up.*

***I give you my own peace and my gift is nothing like the peace of this world. You must not be distressed and you must not be daunted.***
***John 14:27 (Phillips)***

We live in perhaps the most stressful period in human history. Most of us spend a good deal of time being tense, agitated, uptight, strained. Our jaws hurt. Our eyes hurt. Our joints hurt. In the midst of this, Jesus doesn't promise to make the problems go away. He doesn't say there will be no more stress or fatigue. He just says that in the middle of all of this we can know and experience rest. It's like having a refuge in the midst of all the craziness, a retreat center where we can go when life is just too much. It's peace amidst the storm. The eye in the middle of the hurricane. A place of stillness amidst the stress. An oasis. Hope amidst the confusion.

*As a thirsty person needs water, I need Your peace, Jesus. Thank You that Your peace is a promise.*

GIFTS OF COMFORT AND REASSURANCE

*Come to me and I will give you rest—all of you
who work so hard beneath a heavy yoke. Wear
my yoke—for it fits perfectly—and let me teach
you; for I am gentle and humble, and you shall
find rest for your souls; for I give you only
light burdens. Matthew 11:28–30 (TLB)*

While traveling one summer, our family
stopped at a lake for a picnic. The boys and I
decided to go for a swim. I decided just to float
on my back. I completely relaxed . . . let go . . .
let the water hold me. I was at total peace. I let
go of the pain. It seemed like I was "resting" in
the water. The immensity of the lake held me up.

I thought of Jesus' words, "Come to me . . .
and I will give you rest." Jesus didn't say, "Do
this and you will have rest" or "Don't do this,
and you will have rest." He said, "Come to
me . . . and I will give you rest." It is an intimate
relationship He offers.

❖ ——————————— ———————————

*I am tired from the struggle, Lord.
I cling to Your promise of rest.*

❦

*Don't you believe that I am in the Father, and that the Father is in me? . . . And I will do whatever you ask in my name, so that the Son may bring glory to the Father. John 14:10a, 13*

Jesus is God's Son. He used to do all the hard work, like miracles and trying to teach people about God who didn't want to learn. They finally got tired of His preaching and they crucified Him. But He was good and kind like His Father, and He told His Father that they didn't know what they were doing and to forgive them, and God said OK. . . . And now He helps His Father out by listening to prayers. . . . You can pray anytime you want and They are sure to hear you because They've got it worked out so one of them is on duty all the time. . . .

Danny Dunton, 8 years old

❦ _____

*Jesus, like Your disciples, sometimes I'm confused by Your words. But I do understand that you have everything under control.*

*Therefore, whoever humbles himself like this child is the greatest in the kingdom of heaven.*
**Matthew 18:4**

Jesus is encouraging us to stay childlike—wide-eyed, full of wonder, trusting, and humble. To be humble means not to make comparisons. Children have this kind of freedom. They insist, without knowing it, on just being themselves. They take life as it is. Head on, full blast, living to the hilt. They live in the present. They are not overwhelmed by worry or guilt. They take their significance for granted and respond to the world in a wide-open manner.

*Don't let me become bored and jaded, Lord. Keep me wide-eyed and full of wonder.*

◆

*Paul . . . traveled throughout the region of
Phrygia and Galatia, having been kept by the
Holy Spirit from preaching the word in the
province of Asia. Acts 16:6*

Many of the best things that have happened to me came when I found the second right answer. When I graduated Stanford, my first job choice was head coach for the Stanford freshman football team. My second choice was San Francisco Bay area director for Young Life. The coaching job went to the the famous Dick Vermeil. My second choice ended up changing my life.

When the Holy Spirit prevented Paul from speaking God's message in Asia, Paul had a vision of a man saying, "Come over to Macedonia and help us!" Because Paul went to Macedonia (his second choice) God brought the message of the gospel to the whole world.

Look for the second right answer, the third right answer, and maybe the fourth. Like Paul, it could change lives.

◆ _____

*Lord, help me examine even the small decisions of
my life to make sure I'm following Your lead.*

❧

*And they, continuing daily with one accord in the temple, and breaking bread from house to house, did eat their meat with gladness and singleness of heart. Acts 2:46 (KJV)*

We all know quality people whose inner and outer lives seem to match. They are available, uncluttered, and open. They have a oneness with life.

Albert Einstein was famous for his admiration of childlike simplicity. Through his immense powers of wonder and concentration, he changed the world with a simple formula: $E=mc^2$. This formula reminds me of Richard Foster's statement, "Simplicity is not really simple."

If we are wise, our journey through life will be toward that profound simplicity that triumphs over confusion. "To be simple," Dietrich Bonhoeffer said, "is to fix one's eyes solely on the simple truth of God at a time when all concepts are being confused, distorted, and turned upside down."

❧ ——————————————————————

*Integrate my inner and outer life into an uncluttered simplicity that can only come from You.*

❁

*Praise be to the God and Father of our Lord Jesus Christ, who has blessed us in the heavenly realms with every spiritual blessing in Christ. For he chose us in him before the creation of the world to be holy and blameless in his sight. In love he predestined us to be adopted as his sons through Jesus Christ. Ephesians 1:3–5a*

Christianity began as a great adventure. Being a disciple was a tremendous challenge and following Jesus Christ demanded everything. Who would have imagined that such a vision would ever finally become, in the eyes of many, a formal and finished system to be passively received?

Too many of us are still passive observers of the greatest event that mankind has ever known. What on earth could be more important than knowing God personally? If the claims of Christianity are true, then we've got something to celebrate!

❁ _____

*Praise You, God and Father of my Lord Jesus Christ! I celebrate the unmatchable privilege of knowing You!*

❧❧

*For the foolishness of God is wiser than man's wisdom, and the weakness of God is stronger than man's strength. I Corinthians 1:25*

God's plan invariably involves men and women. I'm still amazed and amused when I look around—or even worse, when I look into the mirror—at God's plan. What a risk! It would be obviously impossible if God didn't also send His Holy Spirit to live this plan in us and through us.

It is upon this radical proposition that our faith is based. But what kind of a person does God choose to use? God's choice of material is diametrically opposed to man's. Man chooses an individual on the basis of what he is while God chooses an individual on the basis of what he is to become.

❧❧ _____

*I am grateful that You chose to take a risk on me.*

❖

*O Lord, you alone are my hope; I've trusted you from childhood. Yes, you have been with me from birth and have helped me constantly—no wonder I am always praising you! Psalm 71:5, 6 (TLB)*

In his book *The Healing Choice*, Ron Lee Davis says, "In this life, we will encounter hurts and trials that we will not be able to change. We are just going to have to allow them to change us."

However hopeless they may seem, unsolvable problems offer us a new opportunity to listen to God in brand new ways.

Cradled within the human predicament is the fact that some problems are beyond our ability to resolve, and when we find ourselves struggling with them, we are tormented by anguish, bewilderment, and even disillusionment. We must remember during those dark times what God has taught us during times of the light.

❖ ─────────────────────────

*Help me when the way seems dark, Lord, to remember what You've shown me in the light.*

❧

*Then he said to him, "Follow me!" John 21:19b*

How do we break the spell of gloom and accept the invitation to a life of joy, wonder, rest, and freedom? The first step is to let go of the attitudes that would have us deny our health and happiness in an effort to be responsible. Let go of the fears of inconvenience. Let go of the need to constantly compare. We must refresh ourselves in some of the simple joys of being alive—turn off the TV and experience again the thrill of living our lives directly rather than vicariously.

Breaking the spell requires risk and abandonment. But who ever said it was safe to follow Jesus Christ? He has a way of confronting us in the strangest ways; of popping the balloons that we were hiding behind in order to prove again to us that this abundant life He spoke about is more than just a good idea.

❧ ───────────────────────

*Jesus, I want to follow You with abandon, letting go of whatever holds me back.*

❋

*And God raised us up with Christ and seated us*
*with him in the heavenly realms in Christ Jesus,*
*in order that in the coming ages he might show*
*the incomparable riches of his grace, expressed*
*in his kindness to us in Christ Jesus.*
*Ephesians 2:6, 7*

The American dream of having it all together makes us pretend to be more whole than we really are in the hope that it will invite a greater acceptance from others and somehow heal our loneliness and emptiness. But a loneliness which is not fully embraced and experienced can break us and haunt us. Trying to avoid it only makes it more powerful. The more we run and hide, the more it will pursue us until it finds us and swallows us whole.

Many of us are drowning in our own emptiness, not realizing that this is an invitation to be filled by an ever-present God, a God who loves us more than we will ever understand or experience.

❋ ───────────────────────────────

*I can thank You for my loneliness when I know that*
*You will fill the empty places with Yourself.*

❀

*And a voice came from heaven: "You are my Son, whom I love; with you I am well pleased." At once the spirit sent him out into the desert.*
**Mark 1:11, 12**

Jesus has just been baptized. A holy dove has descended from heaven to endorse Him as the Son of God. The heavens have opened. The place is in awe. Folks are stunned. Excited. Expectant. The Messiah they've been awaiting for centuries has just been announced. Jesus is ready to begin His public ministry. What will God do next?

What God did next was to send Jesus into the wilderness to undergo loneliness, hunger, hardship, and temptation.

Isn't it interesting that the way the Father showed His love for Jesus, His only Son, was to put Him in the desert at the critical beginning of His ministry?

Perhaps one of the reasons God nudges each of us into a desert of some kind is so that we will learn to depend on Him in new ways.

❀ ——————————————————————

*Give me a new perspective on my desert experiences, Father.*

❈

*Whoever drinks the water I give him will never thirst. Indeed, the water I give him will become in him a spring of water welling up to eternal life. John 4:14*

Our devious media have convinced us that love is something that happens to us; thus we are constantly trying to make ourselves appear more lovable. We make up and make over. We work our way up the ladder and we work out. We take vitamins and rub lotions all over our bodies. We try new hairdos, new clothes, and new ideas. We wait and wait for that perfect person or job or situation to come along and make everything all right . . . while countless opportunities slip by us unnoticed.

We are unsatisfied because God Himself can't give us what we think we want, while all this time He wants to give us far more than we can ask or even want to receive.

❈ ─────────────────────────────

*Lord, how often I have concentrated on the outside, and ignored the satisfying, living water You offer me.*

❀

*Therefore do not worry about tomorrow, for tomorrow will worry about itself. Each day has enough trouble of its own. Matthew 6:34*

A friend of mine shared a letter with me that he had received from his parents during a time of particular struggle.

"We have an idea," they wrote, "that God is leading us to a desired goal—He is not. His purpose is that I depend on Him and His power now. If I can stay in the middle of the turmoil, calm and unperplexed, that is the end of God's purpose. God's training is for now. This minute. Not something in the future. God's end is to enable me to see that He can walk on the chaos of my life just now. If we have a further end in view, we do not pay sufficient attention to the immediate. When we realize obedience is the end, then each moment is precious. God never gives strength for tomorrow or the next hour, but only for the strain of the minute."

❀ ───────────────────────

*Thank You for minute-to-minute strength.
It's all I need.*

*Help one another to stand firm in the faith every
day, while it is still called "today."* . . . *For we
continue to share in all that Christ has for us
so long as we steadily maintain until the
end the trust with which we began.*
Hebrews 3:13a, 14 (Phillips)

Sometimes we cherish our dreams but fail
to act to make them happen. So we continually
look to the future for happiness, and our provi-
sional lives right now are filled only with antici-
pation.

We need to constantly emphasize that life,
God's life within us, is happening here and now,
and the paradox is that we must practice the
presence—otherwise it will elude us. My son said
it so well one day when he said, "It's better here,
isn't it, Daddy?" We need to remind each other
often that it is better here, and it is better now.

We are sitting on a miracle, but we don't recognize it—God has given us everything we need
to be happy.

---

*Forgive me for being deaf and blind to all I have in
You right now—everything I need to be truly happy.*

🔹

*As thy days, so shall thy strength be.*
*Deuteronomy 33:25b (KJV)*

As we move closer to God's rhythm for our lives, we realize that He has given us exactly enough time to achieve His purpose for us.

We live in three tenses: past, present, and future. The day is the smallest division of God-given time. Seconds, minutes, and hours are artificial and man-made, but the day is a product of creation—a span of time God has provided.

Every morning brings new mercies and blessings. Said the psalmist, "Blessed be the Lord who daily bears us up" (Psalm 68:19).

A saintly invalid, who was crippled and had to spend the rest of her life in bed, was once asked, "How long must you lie like that?"

She answered, "Just one day at a time." Divine help is never promised for a month or even a week in advance, but only for each day.

🔹 ───────────────────────────

*Every morning brings a new supply of Your mercies and blessings, Father. Great is Your faithfulness to me.*

*Men will praise God for the obedience that
accompanies your confession of the gospel of
Christ, and for your generosity in sharing with
them and with everyone else. And in their prayers
for you their hearts will go out to you, because
of the surpassing grace God has given you.
Thanks be to God for his indescribable gift!
II Corinthians 9:13b–15*

How can a committed person enjoy
leisure amid the tapestry of pain we view on the
evening news each night? Fortunately, Scripture
will not allow us to neutralize its overwhelming
message of grace. For although it is a library of
nations and individuals torn and divided;
although its pages ache with chastening afflic-
tion and despair; these are consistently overpow-
ered by a God of grace. The Bible does not hide
the hollow places of doubt and emptiness, yet it
is very clear in its celebration of life.

*In the midst of a world torn by pain and struggle,
may Your grace come through me.*

*Therefore, there is now no condemnation for those who are in Christ Jesus, because through Christ Jesus the law of the Spirit of life set me free from the law of sin and death.*
**Romans 8:1, 2**

A friend of mine mixed up his words one day and said, "All we have is the past, the pleasant, and the future." We thought it was even a better way to echo a truth that all too many of us miss. Few Christians recognize how radical their posture in the world truly is. Their past is absolutely forgiven and their future is absolutely certain, so that, more than any other body of people on the face of the earth, they are free to live in the "pleasant tense."

*You have set me free to live. Let my living be in the power of Your Holy Spirit.*

❁

*Moreover we know that to those who love God,
who are called according to his plan, everything
that happens fits into a pattern for good.*
*Romans 8:28 (Phillips)*

I prefer detours to the rough road of
through-ness. When given the opportunity, my
tendency is to avoid difficulty rather than facing
it squarely. But we must accept and go through
our difficulties in order to find the kind of
peace, joy, endurance, steadfastness, and indefati-
gable hope that God wants for us in our journey to become more like His Son. His steadfast
promise is His presence in the midst of going
through.

❁ ————————————————————

*I can go through any difficulty when I remember that
You hold the big picture in Your hand.*

❀

*For if the many died by the trespass of the one man, how much more did God's grace and the gift that came by the grace of the one man, Jesus Christ, overflow to the many! Romans 5:15b*

Grace: a worn-out and tired word that people tend to avoid or, worse yet, bounce around flippantly. But the reality is rich, vivid, powerful. Grace: that overexposed and underexperienced gift from beyond, to help us struggle through the dailiness of our time, and perhaps lighten our step and point the way. A glimpse, not just of what life can be, but of what life really is. Grace: a gentle wedge that separates the shadows amidst our crowded and exhausting days. Grace: it is not of reason, but experience—this holy, wonderful, wild, and crazy-beyond-us-yet-within-us life of God.

❀ ————————————————————

*Even a glimpse of Your grace is enough to see me through, gracious God.*

✺

*I tell you the truth, you will weep and mourn while the world rejoices. You will grieve, but your grief will turn to joy. . . . Now is your time of grief, but I will see you again and you will rejoice, and no one will take away your joy.*
*John 16:20, 22*

What but grace could turn our sorrow into a joy that no one can take from us?

Our limitations can become the very invitation to discover fully the dimensions of grace, the improbable path to God's otherwise hidden blessing. God does His good work within us and wants to continue to expand it, not because of who we are, but because of who He is.

That which appears to us to be limitation can actually become our unexpected advantage and asset. As we're forced to our knees once again, we discover the holy and wonder-full gift of life.

✺ ─────────────────────────────

*I bow before You, laying my limitations at Your feet, knowing that Your grace will turn them into a gift.*

❧

*But now the Lord who created you, O Israel,*
*says, Don't be afraid, for I have ransomed you;*
*I have called you by name; you are mine.*
*Isaiah 43:1 (TLB)*

I recently discovered that there are 365 "fear nots" in the Bible. Could it be that it is to remind us daily that we need not fear the difficulties that all of us eventually have to face?

And why should we not fear? Because "*I have called you by name. You are mine.*" Then these comforting words from Isaiah 43:

"When you pass through the waters,

I will be with you; and when you pass through the rivers,

they will not sweep over you.

When you walk through the fire,

you will not be burned;

the flames will not set you ablaze.

Since you are precious and honored in my sight

and because I love you. . . .

Do not be afraid, for I am with you."

❧ ─────────────────────────

*You know my name, Lord, and You have promised to be with me. I will not be afraid.*

🔹

*I no longer call you servants . . . Instead, I have called you friends. John 15:15a*

Leslie Weatherhead tells the story of an old Scot who was ill. When his minister came to call, he noticed a chair pulled close to the bed and said, "Well, Donald, I see I'm not your first visitor of the day."

"Ah," he said. "Let me tell you about that chair. Years ago, I was finding it difficult to pray. When I shared my problem with my pastor he said, 'Just put a chair opposite you, and imagine Jesus sitting in it. Talk to Him as you would a friend.' And that's what I've been doing ever since."

The next day the old man's daughter called their minister to report that her father had died. "I left him sleeping comfortably. When I returned, he had passed away." She paused. "He hadn't moved . . . except that his hand was on the empty chair beside his bed."

🔹 ————————————————————

*Oh my Friend, Jesus, let me walk this life with my hand in Yours, and when it's time, lead me home to You.*

# THE LORD IS MY SHEPHERD

❦

*All Scripture is God-breathed and is useful for
teaching, rebuking, correcting and training
in righteousness. II Timothy 3:16*

You can keep coming back again and
again to certain Scripture you thought you
knew and understood, and be stunned and
refreshed by it in ways you never experienced
before.

For me, one of those Scripture passages is the
Twenty-third Psalm. Kids memorize it; people
on their deathbeds quote from it; plaques frame
it; yellow markers highlight it.

I've read it in virtually every version and in
some foreign languages. I've experienced it
thousands of times, and it has never failed to
excite me, revive me, refresh me, restore me.

What Scripture has God illuminated in your
life? Let it penetrate your thoughts throughout
this day.

❦ _____

*Thank You for those Scripture passages that have
made their imprint on my mind and heart, and are
available to me wherever I am today.*

*I am the good shepherd; I know my sheep and my sheep know me. John 10:14*

Two men were asked to read the Twenty-third Psalm in a service. The first man was a gifted orator. No one had ever heard this famous passage read with such elegance. When he finished, the congregation murmured their approval.

The second man was older and hadn't learned how to project his voice. He had never heard of meter and rhythm. On some words he almost slowed to a stop, as if to savor the fullness of their meaning. There were unmeasured pauses. Then very deliberately he would begin again, emphasizing certain words with a curious power.

When he finished, there was a stunned silence—and then the people stood and responded to his reading with a two-minute standing ovation.

What was the difference? The first man knew the Twenty-third Psalm. The second man knew the Shepherd.

---

*Shepherd of my life, I want to know You better.*

❧

*Taste and see that the Lord is good; blessed is the man who takes refuge in him. Psalm 34:8*

I learned the words to Psalm 23:1 when I was a young child: "The Lord is my shepherd; I shall not want." Now I'm trying to understand the music behind the notes, the resonance beneath the surface, the substance beneath the form. Thirty-one vowels and consonants, shaped into a particular truth that, if properly under-stood and experienced, could reshape our lives.

- The Lord is my shepherd; I shall not want.
- The Lord is my shepherd; therefore, I lack nothing.
- Because the Lord is my shepherd, I have everything that I need.
- The Lord is my shepherd; I shall want nothing.

Each version reminds me in a new way that the Lord is the source, the purpose, the power, the privilege of my existence.

❧ _____

*Lord, You have proven Your goodness.*
*With You I lack nothing.*

*But he said to me, "My grace is sufficient for you, for my power is made perfect in weakness." Therefore I will boast all the more gladly about my weaknesses, so that Christ's power may rest on me. II Corinthians 12:9*

Time and again I come back to that single verse, Psalm 23:1. The Lord is my shepherd; I shall not be in want. I shall not be found lacking. I shall not be left empty or hopeless. I shall not be found wanting. God is consistent in this theme throughout the Bible, and I am practicing to make this principle consistent in my life. The here and now is enough.

Change takes place because we're fully accepted, not because we're strong. Make friends with your weaknesses. Identify five of them and thank God for them. They are opportunities for His power to be displayed in your life today.

*It's hard to thank You for these weaknesses of mine, God. But I do ask that You will use them to display Your power.*

✚

*Praise the Lord. Praise the Lord, O my soul. I will praise the Lord all my life; I will sing praise to my God as long as I live. Psalm 146:1, 2*

Live in the here and now. No matter who you are, or in what wealth or poverty you live, life will not allow you more than one minute at a time. What a blow to our ego—what hope for our souls.

The peace and happiness we seek must begin with an unadorned acceptance of where we are and who we are. God is not only the God of history and of the future, but also very much the God of the now, the God of the process.

Because He is my Lord and Shepherd, I lack nothing. And because of that, I have everything I need to be happy here and now.

✚ ———————————————————————

*I praise You, God, that You are my Shepherd, the Lord of my life.*

❧

*For to me, to live is Christ and to die is gain.*
*Philippians 1:21*

In *I Shall Not Want*, Robert Ketchum tells of a Sunday school teacher who asked her group of children if anyone could quote the entire Twenty-third Psalm. A golden-haired four-and-a-half-year-old girl raised her hand. A bit skeptical, the teacher asked if she could really quote the entire psalm. The little girl came to the rostrum, faced the class, made a perky little bow, and said: "The Lord is my shepherd, that's all I want." She bowed again and went and sat down. That may well be the greatest interpretation I've ever heard.

❧ ———————————————————————

*Forgive me, Lord. So many times I forget that You are all I need. Help me grow in relationship to You until You are all I want.*

❧

*He makes me lie down in green pastures, he leads me beside quiet waters. Psalm 23:2*

Recently I realized that the first sentence of Psalm 23 ties together and is actually the theme of the entire psalm. For example, the Lord is my shepherd; therefore, I shall not want for rest ("He makes me to lie down in green pastures").

In my own life the word that I would have to keep underlining is *makes*. It seems as though the last years have been a process of God's constantly making me lie down, so that I will look up to Him. Making me stop, so that I can hear His voice. As T. S. Eliot says, "In the stillness is the dancing." Perhaps like me, God is teaching you what it means to lie down, to live out of rest. It may mean having to lay down ambitions, dreams, ideas. But the promise is: I shall not want for what is important.

❧ _____

*Oh my Shepherd, create a hunger in my soul for Your rest—no matter what that means for my ambitions and dreams.*

❖

*He restores my soul.*
*Psalm 23:3a*

The Lord is my shepherd; I shall not want for renewal. ("He renews life within me"). God is in the renewal business. One of the most exciting things I know about joy is that it can be restored, no matter how impossible our situation may seem. Psalm 51:12 says: "O Lord, restore me to the joy of thy salvation." Renewal is more than mere repair, more than just knocking out a few dents. It's an inside-out job. The New Testament word for it is *metanoia*, which means to be transformed—completely renewed. In Christ we are new creatures altogether, and this is a continual process, not merely a once-in-a-lifetime thing.

❖ ———————————————————

*Renew Your joy within me. Continue Your work*
*of inner restoration through this day.*

***He guides me in paths of righteousness for his name's sake. Psalm 23:3b***

The Lord is my shepherd; I shall not want." How I long for that kind of absolute surrender.

The Lord is my shepherd; I shall not want for guidance ("And for his name's sake, he guides me in the right path"). I was asked not too long ago what some of my options were in life. For me, it's real simple. As much as I stray, I know that my ultimate goal is simply to have Him guide me on the right path for His name's sake. How do we know if it is the Lord speaking or someone else? The only answer I know is to become very familiar with His voice by spending time alone with Him.

*I need Your guidance, Lord. You've chosen a path for me. Help me stay on it.*

❧

*Even though I walk though the valley of the shadow of death, I will fear no evil, for you are with me; your rod and your staff, they comfort me. Psalm 23:4*

The Lord is my shepherd; I shall not want for courage ("Even though I walk through the valley as dark as death, I fear no evil, for thou art with me; thy staff and thy crook are my comfort"). The longer I live, the more important I believe courage is. The most important level of courage is to accept ourselves solely, when our world bombards us with messages to the contrary. The courage to love ourselves (which is a commandment in Scripture, and not merely a "suggestion") in the midst of all the turmoil and confusion and urgency which pushes and pulls at us each day. And then, the courage to forget ourselves in recklessly loving a hurting world with the genuine love of Christ.

---

*You are my protection and comfort in the dark times. I look to You for courage to reflect Your love to this hurting world.*

*You prepare a table before me in the presence of my enemies. You anoint my head with oil; my cup overflows. Psalm 23:5*

The Lord is my shepherd; I shall not want for joy ("Thou spreadest a table before me in the sight of my enemies. Thou hast richly bathed my head with oil and my cup runs over"). In the Old Testament, oil almost always represents gladness or joy. It was an essential part of many spiritual celebrations. Joy is one of the surest signs of the presence of God, and the promise here is to be bathed in oil to such an extent that our cup runs over.

*Sometimes, God, the joy of living life in fellowship with You bubbles up and overflows my soul. Praise You, Lord!*

***Surely goodness and mercy shall follow me all the days of my life. Psalm 23:6a (KJV)***

The Lord is my shepherd; I shall not want for mercy. It has been said that grace is getting what we don't deserve, and mercy is not getting what we do deserve. When I was younger, mercy was a rather distant word to me. These days it's a very tangible reality. I know myself well enough to realize how much I have fouled up my life and am in need of God's mercy.

---

*Without Your mercy, my situation would be hopeless, Lord.*

❀

***I will dwell in the house of the Lord forever.***
***Psalm 23:6b***

The Lord is my shepherd; therefore, I shall not want forever ("And I will dwell in the house of the Lord forever"). Eternity is a rather long time. Most of our minds are incapable of even starting to comprehend what it means.

I don't think about eternity a lot. But when I do, I'm grateful to know that it's in His hands, and not mine, and that I shall not be found wanting. Eternal life began when the first connection and commitment was made to Jesus Christ. According to the rumor, it has no end. I rather like that.

❀ ——————————————————

*I can't comprehend "forever," but I can comprehend a*
*life with You beyond this one. Thank You*
*that this is not all there is.*

*Your goodness and unfailing kindness shall
be with me all of my life, and afterwards I
will live with you forever in your home.*
*Psalm 23:6 (TLB)*

During an especially difficult year I
received a call from a dear Episcopal friend. He
said, "You evangelicals still all believe that God's
grace and mercy depend on the beauty and the
faithfulness of the believer. They don't." He
reminded me of one of the greatest truths, so
easy to forget—God's mercy depends on His
character, not on ours.

As you experience the difficulties of life, I
simply invite you to remember the promise,
"Goodness and mercy unfailing, these will follow me all the days of my life." The hound of
heaven pursues us recklessly until He can overwhelm us with His mercy, His love, and His
goodness.

*Oh God, if Your grace and mercy depended on my
faithfulness, I would never experience it. How I
thank You that in Your great and unfathomable love,
You are willing to pursue me!*

❀

*If I rise on the wings of the dawn, if I settle on the far side of the sea, even there your hand will guide me. Psalm 139:9, 10*

The Lord is my wilderness guide.
*Therefore I am prepared for anything.*
*In the high meadows*
    *He invites me to rest.*
*He leads me beside a river of stillness*
    *and there He reignites my soul.*
*He joyfully guides me into paths of obedience*
    *for His name's sake.*
*Even though I pass through a valley of darkness*
    *I fear nothing,*
*Because I am in Your presence*
    *Your rod and staff give me strength.*
*You prepare a banquet for me*
    *even amidst my emptiness.*
*You anoint my head with gladness.*
    *My heart overflows.*
*Your presence and mercy constantly preserve*
    *me every day of my life.*
*I now know that my home is where my heart*
    *is—with You, now and each day for eternity.*

❀ _____

*Acknowledgments*

**Looking to the Source of Life,** page 15:
Ron Lee Davis, *Gold in the Making,* Nashville, Thomas
Nelson, 1984, p. 86.

**The Power in Weakness and Pain,** page 52:
Margery Williams, *The Velveteen Rabbit,* New York,
Doubleday and Co., Inc., 1983, pp. 16–17.

**Choose Life!,** page 76:
Victor Frankl, *The Doctor and the Soul,* New York,
Bantam Books, 1952, p. xiii.

Page 87: Lloyd Ogilvie, *Drumbeat of Love,* Waco, Texas,
Word Books, 1976, p. 112.

**In Quietness and Confidence,** page 177:
Mark Link, S.J., *Breakaway,* Allen, Texas, Argus
Communications, 1980, p. 7.

**The Importance of Problems,** page 309:
Jordan Paul and Margaret Paul, *Do I Have to Give Up
Me to Be Loved by You?,* Minneapolis, CompCare
Publications, 1983, p. 10.

This book contains material originally published in
*You Gotta Keep Dancin', When I Relax I Feel Guilty,* and
*Through the Wilderness of Loneliness,* all published by
Chariot Family Publishing. Used by permission.

Pages 28, 39, 107, 179, 206, 227, 245, 246, 286, and 295
are from *Holy Sweat,* by Tim Hansel, © 1987, Word
Inc., Dallas, Texas. All rights reserved. Used by
permission.